"Gentle and wise, these meditations serve as a trusted guide through key scriptures and their legacies. This volume has brought together brilliant authors to dig deep into texts and pull out hidden gems and spiritual insights which will nourish our souls and minds. If you ever wanted your smartest friend to lead you in spiritual reflection, this is it."

—*Kate Bowler, bestselling author of* Everything Happens for a Reason and Other Lies I've Loved

"These brilliant meditations on Scripture testify to the power of historical reflection for supporting the vital work of calling Christian believers to act justly, to love mercy, and to walk humbly with our God. They instruct, chasten, unsettle, and console. Authored by some of today's most thoughtful Christian historians, this collection masterfully displays the integration of keen and learned historical insight with genuine, warm-hearted devotion to Jesus."

—*Jay Green, Professor of History, Covenant College*

"I truly enjoyed these daily devotional readings. Each of these impressively thoughtful historians reflects on an example from their studies that illustrates a biblical principle. This is a particularly fine volume for anyone who appreciates history or is considering why Christians should study history."

—*George Marsden, author of* The Outrageous Idea of Christian Scholarship

Faith

A Devotional
& History

Christopher Gehrz and Beth Allison Barr

editors

1845 BOOKS

Cover and book design by Kasey McBeath

The prayer for Ruth 2 is copyright © 2002, Augsburg Fortress, "Thematic Prayer for 23rd Sunday after Pentecost, Year B," from the Revised Common Lectionary. Used by permission. The prayer for Joel 2:28-32 is copyright © 2002, Augsburg Fortress, "Intercessory Prayer for Pentecost, Year C," from the Revised Common Lectionary. Used by permission. The prayer for Amos 5:10-15 is copyright © 2018, Moody Publishers; John Perkins, *One Blood: Parting Words to the Church on Race and Love.* Used by permission.

Library of Congress Cataloging-in-Publication Data
Names: Barr, Beth Allison, editor. | Gehrz, Christopher, 1975- editor.
Title: Faith and history : a devotional / Beth Allison Barr and Christopher Gehrz, editors.
Description: Waco : 1845 Books, 2020. | Summary: "Christian historians offer reflections on various historical events and figures in light of passages from Scripture, encouraging lay engagement with the past through the lens of religious devotion"-- Provided by publisher.
Identifiers: LCCN 2020020762 (print) | LCCN 2020020763 (ebook) | ISBN 9781481313469 (paperback) | ISBN 9781481313490 (pdf) | ISBN 9781481313476 (epub)
Subjects: LCSH: Devotional literature. | Church history--Miscellanea.
Classification: LCC BV4801 .F35 2020 (print) | LCC BV4801 (ebook) | DDC 242--dc23
LC record available at https://lccn.loc.gov/2020020762
LC ebook record available at https://lccn.loc.gov/2020020763

NATIONAL
ENDOWMENT
FOR THE
HUMANITIES

Faith and History has been made possible in part by a major grant from the National Endowment for the Humanities: NEH CARES. Any views, findings, conclusions, or recommendations expressed in this book do not necessarily represent those of the National Endowment for the Humanities.

The support of the Conference on Faith and History (CFH) board and members made this devotional possible.

WE ARE SO THANKFUL.

Contents

Introduction

Christopher Gehrz and Beth Allison Barr

A fifteenth-century manuscript tells of a woman who cried out to God for help. Her name was Margery Kempe, and she had just been threatened with burning as a heretic. She was all alone and "quaking dreadfully," as chapter 13 of her first book reads. So she did what we would do, what probably you would do, too: "Then she prayed in her heart to our Lord, thinking to herself in this way: 'I came to this place, Lord, for love of you. Blessed Lord help me and have mercy on me.'"

Suddenly, two men appear out of nowhere. They stand beside her and escort her away from the angry crowds. They take her safely home.

We can imagine Margery breathing a sigh of relief, whispering a prayer of gratitude. God whispered back, assuring Margery that his "merciful eyes" are ever watching her. God heard Margery Kempe, a fifteenth-century woman. He heard her faithful prayer, he answered her, and her life was saved.

Knowing this story about Margery Kempe—a story of God's faithfulness to a Christian woman over five hundred years ago—is one of the unexpected advantages of being a historian. Stories like Margery's fill the past, overflowing into our research and touching our modern lives. Margery Kempe prayed as Christians have always prayed, because we believe God hears. Despite the centuries separating us from Margery's medieval world, isn't it comforting to know that the same God who heard Margery listens to us today?

As historians, we find the prayers and stories of faithful believers from the past encouraging, sobering, meaningful, and instructive. They remind us how shared our human experience is. In this book you'll meet not just Margery Kempe but George Herbert, Frederick Douglass, Madeline Southard, Dietrich Bonhoeffer, Billy Graham, Kathryn Kuhlman, and other people from the past who have cried out to God with the same fear, anger, joy, and gratitude that we bring to God today.

As much as the people of the past are like us, they're also unlike us. For the past is a foreign country, where our sisters and brothers in Christ believed and worshipped differently than us as part of societies, cultures, economies, and political systems different from ours. Because they challenge us to see our faith from a different perspective, the stories of Christians from different times and places—as far from us and from each other as fifth-century Ireland and nineteenth-century Burma—are also instructive, meaningful, and encouraging.

And yes, sobering. As you read this book, you'll hear the stories of refugees fleeing religious persecution, civil rights activists struggling against white supremacy, and the traumatized survivors of civil war and genocide. As we study those pasts and listen to those prayers, we learn to walk more humbly, love more fully, and act more justly in our own time.

In many and various ways, the past illuminates our present—and the same is true for our faith. Truly we are "surrounded by so great a cloud of witnesses" that we can "run with perseverance the race that is set before us, looking to Jesus the pioneer and perfecter of our faith" (Heb. 12:1-2).

So we invite you to join the Christian historians who contributed to this devotional, as we journey together through the biblical and historical past, reading God's word in light of the experiences of those made in God's image. For each scriptural passage—each station along our way—we'll share a reflection drawn from our work as historians, suggest questions for individual reflection or small group discussion, recommend resources for further historical study, and close with a short prayer.

We pray that the journey will comfort, challenge, and strengthen you just as it has comforted, challenged, and strengthened us.

The Old Testament

The Stewardship of the Past

Genesis 1–2

Christopher Gehrz

> The LORD God took the man and put him in the garden
> of Eden to till it and keep it.
>
> (Gen. 2:15)

"God, whose farm is all creation, take the gratitude we give." I love
the sentiment of John Arlott's hymn, which has become part of worship at our church. Not just our tithes and other monetary offerings,
but *all* our "crops of your creation . . . are our prayer." Arlott's allu-
sions to agriculture never fail to make me think of the second creation account in Genesis, where God commissions Adam to "till . . .
and keep" the Garden of Eden.

That's a story that probably made immediate sense to my grand-
parents and their Swedish immigrant ancestors; they all spent their
lives tilling and keeping the rich soil of midwestern farmland.
Unfortunately, I'm not even a good gardener. If I don't wait too long
to plant seeds, I start too early. If I don't water plants too little, I soak
them too much.

But if tending physical space doesn't come easily to me, perhaps I
do better at caring for another dimension of Creation: time.

Christians tend to think of "creation care" in terms of air and water, flora and fauna, but Genesis 1 starts with the division of morning from evening and continues day after day for a week. And we're told later in Scripture that nothing "in all creation" can separate us from the Creator's love: neither space ("nor height, nor depth") nor time ("things present, nor things to come") (Rom. 8:38-39).

So how do we "till and keep" time? A Creator who rested on the seventh day of Creation certainly means his people to steward their personal time wisely—such as not acting as if every hour of every day is meant for production or consumption. But it's not just the right use of things present and things to come that's our concern. I think we're also meant to be good stewards of things past.

That is easiest to understand if history is your profession, like the professors, teachers, archivists, and other contributors to this devotional. But all of us can be good stewards of the past. If God has not only made "everything suitable for its time" but "put a sense of past and future into [our] minds" (Eccl. 3:11), then all of us have the innate ability to "till and keep" the past by *remembering* it.

Of course, that's easier said than done. In the book of Deuteronomy, God repeatedly directs his people to "remember" or "not forget." We need similar reminders, for memory erodes as quickly as soil. Even if our remembering powers were no less limited than the rest of our mortal minds and bodies, we might not want to recall pasts that are awkward, embarrassing, complicated, or traumatic. (In Deuteronomy the Israelites mostly need to be reminded to remember that they were slaves.) So we need to commit to practices that prompt us to think back over the past.

That might mean keeping and reviewing artifacts that take us back in time at a mere glance, listen, or touch: photos, recordings, keepsakes. It might mean fixing certain times of the year—holidays, anniversaries—as temporal speed bumps that force us to slow down and look back at where we've been. It might mean being intentional about having conversations with those who are older than us, to let them transfer their memories to succeeding generations. "Remember the days of old, consider the years long past; ask your father, and he will inform you; your elders, and they will tell you," Moses recited before his death (Deut. 32:7).

But just as importantly, we must preserve the past in a way that is inclusive, not exclusive. Unfortunately this is as hard for Christian communities as it is for any other group of people. For example, congregations can be tempted to erect fences around their histories—to tell stories about themselves to themselves, keeping others at a distance. But the healthiest churches will recognize that the past they work hard to preserve is much like the land God promised to the people of Israel: "a land on which you had not labored, and towns that you had not built, and you live in them" (Josh. 24:13).

History is not property to be protected, but a trust to be shared—as we invite each other into the pasts we've tilled and kept.

REFLECTION AND DISCUSSION

1. When do you struggle most to "remember the days of old, consider the years long past"?
2. What do you already do to "tend and keep" memories of the past? Do those practices make it easier or harder for you to share your stories with others?

FURTHER STUDY

One of my favorite theological reflections on time, history, and memory is *Why Study the Past? The Quest for the Historical Church* by Rowan Williams, the former Archbishop of Canterbury.

PRAYER

O God, you make grass and plants to grow, that we may bring forth food from the earth and wine to gladden our hearts. Help us also to till and keep your good gift of time, that we may live patiently and generously as a people of memory. Amen.

(Adapted from Ps. 104:14-15)

"You See Me"

Genesis 16

Amy L. Poppinga

> So she named the LORD who spoke to her, "You are El-roi"; for she said, "Have I really seen God and remained alive after seeing him?"
>
> (Gen. 16:13)

Having been cast out to the desert in what should have been a guaranteed date with death, we find in the story of Hagar a miraculous encounter with God. Alone and forgotten, Hagar has taken refuge from the harsh desert landscape at a well when she is addressed by an "angel of the Lord" who offers comfort in the midst of her despair. In response to this holy confrontation, Hagar cries out, claiming God as El-roi, "the one who sees." Hagar, in turn, gives a name to this place, calling it the "Well of the Living One who sees me." Eugene Peterson interprets verse 13 this way: "She answered God by name, praying to the God who spoke to her, 'You're the God who sees me! Yes! He saw me; and then I saw him!'"

Who was Hagar to think *she* could name God? This slave woman, with no autonomy or status; a victim of a flawed human attempt to try and speed up God's delayed promise. What a brave act! Her response is one of shock, implying she had no expectation of surviving such an encounter. Does it suggest the desperation of someone with nothing left to lose? Is she all too aware that any changes in her circumstances are beyond her control? The author of Genesis does not imply that Hagar was given immediate relief from her plight after this moment. There was no rescue coming. Instead, Hagar returns to a horrible situation, and life does not get better.

However, Hagar's solace was found in her experience of "being seen" by God. Despite her lowly status, God had not been *indifferent* to Hagar's plight, and the recognition of her suffering was as life-giving as the water in that well. It was an immediate comfort and an assurance she would call upon again on another fateful day in the desert.

As a teacher and Christ-follower, I appreciate so much in Hagar's story. Each fall I teach a course on Middle Eastern history to Christian students. It is rewarding work but exhausting. I warn students at the beginning of the semester that the content can be overwhelming for what it requires of us emotionally and spiritually, as Christians living in the twenty-first-century United States. Students are challenged and convicted when learning of the historical fracturing of the Middle East, with wounds that are still fresh. They struggle with how to reconcile the relative safety and security of their lives when compared against the heartbreaking Syrian refugee crisis or the ongoing instability in Iraq. "Ugh," a student confessed recently, "I kind of wish I just didn't know this stuff. It's easier to just not think about it." Another remarked, "I feel helpless. I mean, what can we possibly do?"

There is no easy answer for these questions, and I do not try and offer one. My students are right. I often feel this way, too. It is much easier to be ignorant. If we do not know about the suffering of others, then at least we do not have to bear the guilt of having chosen to remain indifferent.

In his historic speech on the perils of indifference, Elie Wiesel observes:

> Of course, indifference can be tempting—more than that, seductive.
> It is so much easier to look away from victims. It is so much easier to

avoid such rude interruptions to our work, our dreams, our hopes. It is, after all, awkward, troublesome, to be involved in another person's pain and despair. Yet, for the person who is indifferent, his or her neighbor are of no consequence. And, therefore, their lives are meaningless. Their hidden or even visible anguish is of no interest. Indifference reduces the Other to an abstraction.

How do we prevent indifference? How should believers in El-roi respond? This can take many forms but, as a historian, I am called professionally and personally to avoid indifference by actively choosing to *see*, to humbly bear witness to the plight of the Other. The classroom provides me with a space to create room to care for the stories of those who are suffering. I must develop in my students and myself a commitment to engage what ethicist Martha Nussbaum calls a *narrative imagination*—the willingness to develop compassion toward the Other by imagining life from their perspective. The classroom is a place where the Other must be heard and seen and, beyond that, lifted up. Those who have historically been overlooked or marginalized are seen by God, and despite our often real feelings of paralysis, we must choose to see. This is an act of love for humanity and an expression of love for God.

This is not an easy task. Wiesel warns, "Indifference is always the friend of the enemy, for it benefits the aggressor—never his victim, whose pain is magnified when he or she feels forgotten." The classroom provides a space for my students that can make sure the Other is not forgotten, not abandoned. We may not be immediately able to bring relief or rescue, but we can do the essential work of listening. We can offer the compassionate response, "We see you, too."

REFLECTION AND DISCUSSION

1. Why is being forgotten so painful? Have you ever found comfort or solace in "being seen"?
2. How do you respond to Wiesel's framing of indifference? Do you agree that followers of Christ bear a greater responsibility regarding indifference?

3. How can we be sure "seeing" and "listening" are not just a form of placating? How do we determine when we need to do more for those in suffering?

FURTHER STUDY

Learn more about the significance of Hagar in the three Abrahamic traditions by reading *Hagar, Sarah, and Their Children: Jewish, Christian, and Muslim Perspectives*, edited by Phyllis Trible and Letty M. Russel. The full audio and transcript of Elie Wiesel's historic speech on "The Perils of Indifference" (1999) can be found at https://www .americanrhetoric.com/speeches/ewieselperilsofindifference.html.

PRAYER

El-roi, thank you for seeing me. You have seen my pain; you have sat with me in my sorrow. May I have eyes like yours to see the suffering around me. Help me not to be indifferent. Help me not to give in to my own discomfort or fatigue. Show me, El-roi, who needs to be seen by me: How can I make them feel known? With whom do I need to sit and listen? Help your children to know they are not forgotten.

The Work of Holy Women

Exodus 1:15-22

Lisa Weaver-Swartz

> The king of Egypt said to the Hebrew midwives, one of whom was
> named Shiphrah and the other Puah, "When you act as midwives
> to the Hebrew women, and see them on the birthstool, if it is a
> boy, kill him; but if it is a girl, she shall live." But the midwives
> feared God; they did not do as the king of Egypt commanded
> them, but they let the boys live.
>
> (Exod. 1:15-17)

The sermon text came from the first chapter of Exodus. I listened
as the man behind the pulpit narrated Moses' early life, including
Pharaoh's attempt to kill all infant Hebrew boys. The pastor briefly
chronicled the role of the Hebrew midwives, the women used by
God to spare these children. The sermon went on to focus on Moses'
posture toward God, but I stopped listening. I was captivated,
instead, by the remarkable women in this story.

As a feminist scholar, I'm well aware that the Bible is heavily
androcentric, or male-centered. But this passage is thick with female
agency. Before the people of Israel can be delivered from bondage, a
mother must formulate a subversive and dangerous plan to save her
child, a sister must be willing to carry it out, and a princess must be

able to see outside of her father's power and find in herself the motivation to preserve life. All of them must do these things knowing that their choices could mean death. And yet they act.

The true heroes of this story are the Hebrew midwives. Two of them are named: Shiphrah and Puah. It would have been so easy for them to simply follow orders and carry out the genocide. There likely would have been rewards for their compliance. Or perhaps they might have fled the terrible assignment. But these women chose a remarkable third way. They recognized that Pharaoh and his men would have no knowledge of—or interest in—the physical details of childbirth. But Shiphrah and Puah knew this experience intimately. As Hebrew women, they knew what it was like to live at the intersection of slavery and patriarchy. They knew the joy and beauty of bringing life into the world and the anguish of mothers forced to grieve the death of their children.

Feminist scholars call this "women's standpoint." Because women's lives are framed by gendered and patriarchal structures, they hold knowledge and wisdom that men do not. Their understanding of the world is birthed from experience on the margins. This knowledge is incredibly valuable—not only to women themselves, but to communities, families, and societies. Women have often been the ones to nurture the sick, comfort the distressed, and tend the broken. One of the great gifts of women's standpoint is its drive to preserve life, contradicting masculine inclinations toward warfare and violence. This standpoint is exactly what Shiphrah and Puah employed centuries before feminist theory arrived on the scene. In shifting the conversation toward their own knowledge rather than trying to compete with Pharaoh's, they transformed the story. They even managed to confound the despot without accelerating violence.

There is a contemporary lesson in Shiphrah and Puah's story, too. In a lifetime of church and Sunday School attendance, I've heard the story told countless times, but the emphasis has always been on Moses, the reluctant leader who was transformed into God's mouthpiece as he stood up to Pharaoh to lead the people out of bondage.

The women of Moses' early life appeared only as useful support staff. Moses *led*, they *obeyed*. Moses *acted*, but they were (passively) *used by God*. Perhaps if my pastor had been given the opportunity to learn about women's standpoint, if his seminary education had included the voices of women trained to recognize the value in their own experiences, he might have considered Scripture through the perspectives of Shiphrah and Puah. They were not merely the support staff. Their bravery easily matched Moses', perhaps even surpassing his—since Moses, unlike the midwives, required a heart-to-heart with God before he found the strength to appear before Pharaoh.

Like our Sunday School stories and sermons, our historical memories rarely acknowledge women's standpoint, even when they highlight women as characters. Contemporary scholars and storytellers have the great privilege of working to recover this standpoint. As the story of Moses' early life reminds us, the *way* we tell a story matters. Turning to women's standpoint can illuminate God's powerfully subversive work throughout human history, even in stories we think we already know. It can remind us of God's tendency to begin the work of redemption not through force and power, but through life-giving compassion for those on the margins. It is a standpoint our violent, fearful world craves.

REFLECTION AND DISCUSSION

1. How have you benefitted from women's standpoint on your own personal journey?
2. How do our contemporary faith communities fail to acknowledge the gift of women's standpoint? How might we do better?

FURTHER STUDY

On recovering women's standpoint in the practice of history, see Catherine A. Brekus, *The Religious History of American Women: Reimagining the Past*. To read the Bible with an eye to the experience of women and others on the margins, try Phyllis Trible, *Texts of Terror: Literary-Feminist Readings of Biblical Narratives* and Miguel De La Torre, *Reading the Bible from the Margins*.

PRAYER

God of Shiphrah and Puah, forgive our blindness to your work. Teach us to see through your eyes, to look less to the strong and powerful, and to prioritize the marginalized, the oppressed, and the ignored. Retune our hearts to the surprising rhythms of your holy work, and equip us to pursue this work together. Amen.

Of Bells and Pomegranates

Exodus 28:31-43

Elesha Coffman

> On its lower hem you shall make pomegranates of blue, purple,
> and crimson yarns, all around the lower hem, with bells of gold
> between them all around—a golden bell and a pomegranate
> alternating all around the lower hem of the robe. Aaron shall
> wear it when he ministers, and its sound shall be heard when he
> goes into the holy place before the LORD, and when he comes out,
> so that he may not die.

> (Exod. 28:33-35)

George Herbert (1593–1633), poet and famed orator, was seized
with terror when he made a midlife career switch to ministry in
the Church of England. He tried to back out of his first call to a tiny
church in Bemerton, near Salisbury, but the bishop told him that to
refuse the commission would be a sin, and in any case, a tailor was
on his way to fit Herbert for his vestments. After ringing the church
bell on his first day, he lingered so long in the sanctuary that his
friends waiting outside got worried. Somebody peeked in the window and saw him lying facedown before the altar. On the process
of starting ministry, Herbert wrote that he "endured such spiritual
conflicts as none can think, but only those that have endured them."

Like a professor whose worries about the first day of class manifest as a question about what to wear, some of Herbert's anxiet-
ies attached themselves to his vestments. He wrote a poem titled
"Aaron" that began:

> Holinesse on the head,
> Light and perfections on the breast,
> Harmonious bells below, raising the dead
> To leade them unto life and rest.
>   Thus are true Aarons drest.
>
> Profanenesse in my head,
> Defects and darknesse in my breast,
> A noise of passions ringing me for dead
> Unto a place where is no rest.
>   Poore priest thus am I drest.

Beyond first day jitters, Herbert pretty clearly suffered from depression. In another poem, "Deniall," he wrote one of the saddest lines
in the English language: "O that thou shouldst give dust a tongue /
To crie to thee, / And then not heare it crying!"

Since encountering that line as an English major in college, I have
never been able to read it without tears. But I choked it out in my last
chapel sermon before a career switch from seminary to university
teaching, because I wanted to give my students Herbert as a model
and friend. He had been a country pastor, as most of them were
training to be. He had been depressed, as an estimated one in six
Americans—and as many as one in three American pastors—would
be at some point in their lives. (The figure for American college
students is about one in five; for American college professors it is
unknown, but based on studies in other countries perhaps double
the student rate.) And he expressed those dark feelings in words,
unlike the majority of American pastors, who admit on surveys that
they rarely or never address mental illness in any public setting.

Reading sad poems is not magically going to solve these deep,
deep problems. But Herbert's rich articulations of depression,
among other feelings and visions, create imaginative bridges from
soul to soul, and from souls to God. Modern Americans need those

imaginative bridges, even need the exotic picture of Aaron's vestments in Exodus 28, because, as Walter Brueggemann wrote for *The New Interpreter's Bible*, "This text asserts, against both ideological religious certitude and against confident secularism, that there is a sacramental foundation that makes life possible, that defines life in certain ways, and that precludes the destructiveness and despair that seem so potent among us." Ancient, strange beauty wields power.

Through some holy mystery, the bells and pomegranates on Aaron's robes preserved his life for ministry. Combining that mental image with faith in Jesus Christ got Herbert off the floor of his church, too. He ended his poem:

> So holy in my head,
> Perfect and light in my deare breast,
> My doctrine tun'd by Christ, (who is not dead,
> But lives in me while I do rest)
> Come people; Aaron's drest.

REFLECTION AND DISCUSSION

1. When was the last time you heard someone in church or academic leadership address mental illness in an especially helpful way? An especially unhelpful way?
2. What space is there for strange beauty in your church, or in your classroom?

FURTHER STUDY

George Herbert's works are available for free online in multiple locations, including the Christian Classics Ethereal Library (ccel .org/h/Herbert). *The Temple* contains his poems, while *A Priest to the Temple* offers his down-to-earth advice for parish ministry.

PRAYER

> In so much dregs the quintessence is small:
> The spirit and good extract of my heart
> Comes to about the many hundredth part.
> Yet Lord restore thine image, heare my call:
> And though my hard heart scarce to thee can groane,
> Remember that thou once didst write in stone.

(From George Herbert, "The Sinner")

On the Pleasure of Earning, and the Discipline of Extending This Pleasure

Leviticus 19:9-13

Janine Giordano Drake

> When you reap the harvest of your land, you shall not reap to the
> very edges of your field, or gather the gleanings of your harvest.
> You shall not strip your vineyard bare, or gather the fallen grapes
> of your vineyard; you shall leave them for the poor and the alien:
> I am the LORD your God.

> (Lev. 19:9-10)

There is hardly a greater human pleasure than to feast on the fruits
of your own work. After years of hard labor, followed by years of
wandering in the desert, the first generations of settled Israelites
had begun to earn themselves a nice fortune from fertile land. It
must have been very tempting to believe that they had *earned* all this
newfound wealth by their own grit and determination. Surely some
suggested that godly "financial stewardship" involves squeezing out
the maximum return on a harvest. And yet, while the Lord our God
wanted to bless his people with good harvests and a modicum of
financial stability, his commands in Leviticus demand a particular
discipline with regard to moneymaking that I think we all ought to
dwell upon.

In this passage God issues an explicit command to the Jews to go out of their way to financially support the disabled, foreigners, and the poor. He first tells them to hold back from a complete harvest because the excess of the wealthy is the *property* of the poor. To maximize your own wealth at the expense of the poor constitutes "theft." The Lord God elaborates, "You shall not revile the deaf or put a stumbling block before the blind" (Lev. 19:14). I read that to say that God's people are not to heap any further burdens upon those who struggle to support themselves. We are to help shoulder the burdens of migrants, people with disabilities, and the impoverished not only by offering them good, well-paying jobs but, while they are still poor and struggling, we should invite the poor into our lives and allow them the same *pleasure of earning their own provisions* that God has granted us.

It is worth considering the alternative ways that God could have asked his people to support the poor. They could have been asked to gather the full extent of their harvest and then to distribute an arbitrary 3-6% of it with saccharine notes about the Lord and half-hearted invitations to the poor to join them at the Temple. Why did God not set parameters on how much food left on the vines was overly magnanimous and thereby inefficient, and how much gleaning was unduly parsimonious? Wouldn't that make it easier to obey? I don't think so. Offering provisions is not the only goal of this command. God offers no particular stipulation on the fraction of a harvest that belongs to the poor, but he does say that a fraction of the harvest *belongs* to the poor and to withhold it constitutes *theft*.

One way to interpret this is to note that God is asking his provisioned people to cultivate a disposition of responsibility toward their neighbors who were often poor, sojourners, disabled, and dependent on the rich for jobs. The wealthy are to become attentive to their neighbors' needs and pay them enough to support themselves. God makes no distinction between "fair wages" and "charity." Rather, God labels as a "fair wage" whatever combination of wages and gleaning it takes to support the poor. What I read in this passage is an astute observation about the human condition: that part of what constitutes a "fair wage" is the *pleasure* of feeling like you have earned your own provisions. The provisioned people of God were asked literally to leave money (food) in the fields so that the poor could take the same joy as the financially stable in *earning*, or gathering, the fruits of their own hard labor.

As a labor and working-class historian, I could tell you endless stories about how this passage has been used. It has been a proof text for Christian claims to communism, to stateless agrarian socialism, and to free market capitalism. However, some of these debates miss the point. The ringing message of this passage to me, both as a Christian and as a historian of industrial capitalism, is that support for a living wage and for the welfare of your neighbors is a spiritual discipline.

Like any other spiritual discipline, it appears ritualistic and wasteful at first. However, the more it becomes habitual, the more it changes our understanding of ourselves in relation to our worldly possessions. The temptation to maximize our wealth and call it "well deserved" is human. We need to continually extend to our neighbors the pleasure of working hard, under just and honest circumstances, and the opportunity to earn a provision we can all agree is "well deserved."

REFLECTION AND DISCUSSION

1. A few large companies, including Walmart, Chick-fil-A, and Hobby Lobby, like to identify themselves as Christian corporations. How could the boards of directors of these organizations follow through on the commands of Leviticus 19?

2. Some historians have argued that the New Deal was the brainchild of Fr. John Ryan, the Catholic priest who popularized the principle that all people deserve the opportunity to support themselves through their own hard work. However, in Europe and elsewhere, the idea of Universal Basic Income (UBI) has been eclipsing twentieth-century "jobs programs" as a better method to support the poor, migrants, and the disabled. Does this passage offer insight on the debate between jobs programs and UBI?

FURTHER STUDY

On Father Ryan (whose book on *A Living Wage* was first published in 1906), see the biography by Francis Broderick, *Right Reverend New Dealer*. On Christianity and capitalism, read Bethany Moreton, *To Serve God and Walmart: The Making of Christian Free Enterprise* and Darren Grem, *The Blessings of Business: How Corporations Shaped Conservative Christianity*.

PRAYER

Lord Jesus, help us to dignify the needs and wants of our neighbors, especially those who do not look like us. Help us to remember that all our material blessings come from above. Help us to remember that our neighbors deserve not just enough to live on, but the satisfaction of supporting themselves from the sweat of their own hands and minds. We pray that you would help those of us who have much to leave money on the table for the poor. Would that all of us could practice this spiritual discipline enough that we call alms for the poor not "charity" but a "living wage."

Care for Strangers

Leviticus 19:33-34

Lisa Clark Diller

> When an alien resides with you in your land, you shall not
> oppress the alien. The alien who resides with you shall be to you
> as the citizen among you; you shall love the alien as yourself, for
> you were aliens in the land of Egypt: I am the LORD your God.
>
> (Lev. 19:33-34)

It's hard to be a stranger. I have lived for extended periods of time
in both the United Kingdom and Australia. Even in these English-
speaking countries, I was deeply aware of my foreignness, my dependence on my hosts. While I was a legal and legitimately employed
immigrant in a hospitable nation, my rights and privileges were
definitely not the same as those of a citizen. The mandate to love and
treat the alien equally is a challenging one for us all, even when we
aren't crossing the deep chasms of language and cultural heritage.

In 1685, even as ideas of religious toleration were spreading
throughout Europe, the absolutist monarch of France, Louis XIV,
revoked the Edict of Nantes. If not equality, the Edict had allowed
some religious freedom for French Protestants, known as Huguenots. But Louis' action forced tens of thousands of his Protestant
subjects to leave the country of their birth and ancestry and find

shelter in other places. The influx of Huguenot migrants to the Netherlands and England during the next fifteen years gave us the English word "refugee."

It also gave the British their first modern experience with integrating large numbers of people with a different language and citizenship background. They were deeply sympathetic to these victims of "popish tyranny," as it was framed at the time. However, the Huguenots were also French, the traditional enemy of the British—and many of them were also economic competitors in the cloth industry. There was definite suspicion of these newcomers who spoke no English, and the Huguenots faced efforts to move them along or limit their numbers. While the British state was vital in providing both support and a path to citizenship for these refugees, it was in churches that English and French Christians worked out the most helpful, comforting, and vigorous charitable activities to welcome the "Protestant stranger," as the Huguenots were often called.

What allows us to sympathize with the strangers among us? For the British, it was the Protestant-ness that called out charity for the French among them. The common concern about victims of Catholic oppression allowed them to bypass their traditional suspicion of the French, and even to see a way toward integrating them in Britain's nascent empire. For some of us today, it might be common faith commitments that engage fellow feeling, and if we belong to a denomination with global ties, those sympathies can extend far beyond our cultural boundaries.

But our trust in a God who has told us that there will be enough, who called his people to love aliens who might not serve him but who lived among them, should push us to something more.

For the Huguenots, the grudging welcome they received saved their lives and communities, and it was informed by the call of Leviticus to welcome the stranger. When we find "hooks" of humanity in the aliens around us that allow us to bond with them, we can begin to fulfill the biblical challenge of loving the stranger as ourselves.

REFLECTION AND DISCUSSION

1. What strangers are around you, and how might you begin to love them as yourself?
2. What tempts us to fear the alien among us? What stories from the past might provide models for how that fear could be channeled more productively?

FURTHER STUDY

Recent histories of the Huguenots include Geoffrey Treasure's *The Huguenots* and Jon Butler's *The Huguenots in America*. For information on immigration in the United States, *Coming to America* by Betsy Maestro is a great children's book. To give young readers a more comprehensive survey of this subject, try Linda Barrett Osborne's *This Land Is Our Land: A History of American Immigration*.

PRAYER

God of the Outcast, we pray for protection for those fleeing persecution or hardship. We ask for room in our hearts to welcome them and to love them as ourselves. We thank you for guiding us when we have been strangers. Teach us to trust that your Providence is enough. Amen.

Stones of Memory

Joshua 4

Darin D. Lenz

> Joshua said to them, "Pass on before the ark of the LORD your God into the middle of the Jordan, and each of you take up a stone on his shoulder, one for each of the tribes of the Israelites, so that this may be a sign among you. When your children ask in time to come, 'What do those stones mean to you?' then you shall tell them that the waters of the Jordan were cut off in front of the ark of the covenant of the LORD. When it crossed over the Jordan, the waters of the Jordan were cut off. So these stones shall be to the Israelites a memorial forever."

> (Josh. 4:5-7)

In June 2017 a colleague and I led a group of Fresno Pacific University students, alumni, and friends on a five hundredth Anniversary of the Reformation tour of Switzerland, France, and Germany. When we arrived in Zurich, Switzerland, we toured the historic Grossmünster church where Ulrich Zwingli was once the people's preacher, leading the city into the tumultuous era of the Reformation. What struck me as we walked through Grossmünster was that this was a place where two major streams of the Reformation developed and diverted, with disastrous consequences for one.

Throughout the city of Zurich there were plenty of references to the Swiss Reformed tradition initiated by Zwingli and carried on by his successor Heinrich Bullinger. But what about those who dissented from their leadership and paid with their lives? Conrad Grebel, George Blaurock, and Felix Manz were the first Anabaptists to contend that Christians should follow Christ's example in the New Testament by abandoning infant baptism and practicing adult believer's baptism. Zwingli and the city council were so incensed by their radical reading of the New Testament that persecution soon followed.

On January 5, 1527, Felix Manz was the first Anabaptist to be condemned to death in Zurich. To mock his (re)baptism, Manz was bound and drowned in the middle of the River Limmat—a stone's throw from the Grössmunster. One might think that the memory of someone like Manz would be widely known in Zurich, but the city filled with beautiful churches and their heaven-reaching spires had for centuries ignored the persecution of Anabaptists that occurred during the Reformation era. In the sixteenth century, thousands of Anabaptists throughout Europe would suffer death at the hands of Protestants and Roman Catholics for their radical commitment to their biblically based beliefs.

Since Fresno Pacific University is a Mennonite Brethren institution, there was a desire in our group to acknowledge what Manz had suffered and see the place of his martyrdom. For the people of Israel and the Anabaptists of Zurich, a river was the place of God's work. But unlike the Jordan, the Limmat was not a site of deliverance and hope but one of perseverance and death. By all accounts Manz remained steadfast in his Anabaptist beliefs until his death. The site of Manz' execution is acknowledged on a stone marker just down and on the opposite bank of the river from Grossmünster church. We could stand and see the marker and the river where he died with the magnificent church in the background. With that troubling image in our minds, we recalled the murder of Manz and other Anabaptists in Zurich and prayed for peace and unity among Christians.

Unlike the people of Israel, who immediately set to work remembering what God had done in their crossing over the Jordan River by piling up stones of memory, no historical monument to com-memorate Manz' death was even a possibility for centuries. Not until 2004, the five hundredth anniversary of Bullinger's birth, was a stone marker placed along the bank of the Limmat to recognize where Manz and other Anabaptists were murdered. The installation of the memorial was part of an effort to bring about reconciliation and forgiveness among the descendants of the Swiss Reformed churches and the Swiss Anabaptists. Just like the stones piled up by the Israelites were to be a place of memory for their children, their grandchildren, and their great-grandchildren, this stone marker is a place to remember those who suffered persecution at the hands of other Christians. The marker also serves as a place of sorrow, a place to seek forgiveness and reconciliation, and a reminder that over the centuries Christians and churches have often failed to live out Christ's love and compassion.

Because Christianity is rooted in remembering what Jesus Christ accomplished through his death on the cross and his resurrection, Christians are obligated to remember and tell others about the faith we have inherited over the centuries. All Christians should be historians of their faith: like the Israelites remembering the crossing of the Jordan River, we need to tell our children and grandchildren about how our predecessors lived out their faith. Our past contains painful and disappointing stories that should teach humility, forgiveness, and compassion. By recounting such heartbreaking events, we should forever be aware that God works out his plan through the Holy Spirit despite the frailty and failure of Christians. We must remember and rely on the Holy Spirit to guide us daily so we, too, do not leave a legacy of sorrow, division, and persecution for future generations of Christians.

REFLECTION AND DISCUSSION

1. What is your story of faith since becoming a Christian? What are the ups and downs of that story? Who should you share that story with?

2. Do you know the story of your church or denominational tradition? How might that knowledge help you further your understanding of your everyday faith and practice?

FURTHER STUDY

The story of the early Anabaptists is not widely understood by Christians even though many Christians practice adult believers' baptism in their local congregations and have been shaped by other Anabaptist ideas. George H. Williams' *The Radical Reformation* and C. Arnold Snyder's *Following in the Footsteps of Christ* offer insightful accounts of Anabaptist history, theology, and practice.

PRAYER

Lord Jesus, thank you for what you accomplished through your death and resurrection, and help us to remember every day what you did to save us from our sins. Allow us to recollect all that you have done over the centuries to preserve your Church. Help us to remember our history so that we can rejoice in your faithfulness and seek forgiveness and reconciliation for our unfaithfulness. Let the Holy Spirit guide us in our everyday lives so that we may tell present and future generations about the hope of your eternal promise and the peace of knowing you as Savior. Amen.

Waiting for Harvest

Ruth 2

Brenda Thompson Schoolfield

So she kept close to the young women of Boaz, gleaning until the end of the barley and wheat harvests. And she lived with her mother-in-law.

(Ruth 2:23, ESV)

Widowed and childless, Ruth left Moab to follow her mother-in-law, Naomi, to Israel. She did not have to leave Moab. Naomi's advice to both of her daughters-in-law indicates that both women most likely had prospects in Moab to marry again, to leave behind the sadness of their husbands' deaths and Naomi's own sense of punishment from God for having left the promised land. Ruth's decision is based on more than affection for Naomi. Ruth's pledge is founded on identification with Naomi's people and with their God; Ruth promised loyalty to Jehovah, not just to Naomi and Israel.

We know Ruth's story well. She supported herself and Naomi by gleaning in the fields, as poor women did. She caught Boaz' attention. Eventually they married and Ruth bore a son, Obed, who became the grandfather of King David.

Ruth's journey to Israel and her place in King David's family tree involved a process of commitment and change. Her challenges included barriers created by her language, her sex, her widowhood, her childless state, and her status as a stranger in Israel. She had to learn the language and customs of her new home. She submitted to Naomi's instruction and worked faithfully in the fields. In the end Ruth gained a marriage that healed Elimelech's family line and provided for Ruth and Naomi. Ruth's widowhood and barren state ended through the beautiful picture of redemption.

While Boaz was a redeemer, a type of savior, Ruth was not a hapless damsel in distress. She took on her responsibilities as a daughter to Naomi with determination and humility. She worked with a purpose—to provide food for their household and to maintain the family's reputation in Bethlehem. She committed herself to following Jehovah, God of Israel, and left the gods of Moab behind. She observed and learned how to work alongside the other women. She accepted Naomi's guidance and Boaz' advice. Boaz acknowledged that God would bless her work: "The LORD repay you for what you have done, and a full reward be given you by the LORD, the God of Israel, under whose wings you have come to take refuge" (Ruth 2:12, ESV).

The determination and humility we see in Ruth are different words for characteristics prized in good students: a good work ethic and a teachable spirit. In my university teaching, I teach a large number of first- and second-year students in a Western civilization history course required for all bachelor's degree programs. I spend time encouraging the students to develop habits of learning that will serve them throughout life. I exhort them to work diligently, to bear their work in patience (humility is another way to put that), and to trust that God will bless their efforts. Many of these students find themselves in a strange land (college), leaving home to face the future as adults.

Neuroscientists tell us that learning causes changes in the brain itself. The brain grows new neural pathways, making new connections and reconfiguring itself. These changes happen over time, with engagement in the new activity or with the new information. Learning, then, is much like physical exercise or studying a new musical instrument. A person cannot cram for a history test any more than she can cram for a race or a recital.

I also compare learning to growing vegetables. I cannot plant, water, and fertilize in one weekend, expecting tomatoes by Monday. Similarly, a semester's worth of work cannot happen the night before the final. The semester's end is a type of harvest.

The barley and wheat harvests last approximately four months—about the length of one semester. What Ruth determined to do—to keep house and provide food for her and Naomi—involved a firm commitment, daily discipline, diligent work, and a humble desire to learn. While marriage may not have been Ruth's projected harvest, she did reap rewards for her work. She had food for the table and goodwill in the community. Learning at university requires similar commitment, discipline, work, and humility. The rewards students reap are not merely in the grades they earn but also in the habits and attitudes that will support their learning throughout life.

Ruth's story encourages us to cultivate the attributes of diligence and humility. These characteristics continue to develop and bear fruit over a lifetime. Ruth's trust in Jehovah to provide for her while she did what she could in her situation led her to many blessings.

REFLECTION AND DISCUSSION

1. How are Ruth's challenges different from and similar to the ones you face today?
2. What harvest are you expecting from what you are learning now?

FURTHER STUDY

Esther Lightcap Meek's short book *A Little Manual for Knowing* offers a humane and Christian examination of how we know and learn. There are several good commentaries on the book of Ruth: Carolyn Custis James' *The Gospel of Ruth: Loving God Enough to Break the Rules* and Robert L. Hubbard's *The Book of Ruth* are good starting points.

PRAYER

Providing God, you journeyed with Ruth when her life was burdened by grief. Grant us faith to believe you will provide a future where we see none, that bitterness may turn to joy and barrenness may bear life. Amen.

(Adapted from a Revised Common Lectionary prayer. Copyright © 2002 Consultation on Common Texts. Augsburg Fortress. Used by permission.)

Give We Sense

1 Kings 3:1-12

Joel Carpenter

> "Give your servant therefore an understanding mind to govern
> your people, able to discern between good and evil; for who can
> govern this your great people?" It pleased the Lord that Solomon
> had asked this. God said to him, "Because you have asked this,
> and have not asked for yourself long life or riches, or for the life
> of your enemies, but have asked for yourself understanding to
> discern what is right, I now do according to your word. Indeed
> I give you a wise and discerning mind; no one like you has been
> before you and no one like you shall arise after you."

(1 Kgs. 3:9-12)

A dozen years ago, my wife and I and some friends were visiting
fellow Christians in the West African country of Sierra Leone. We
headed to Kabala, an up-country town in the north, to visit people
in our sister churches there. It was an unforgettable visit, sweet with
fellowship and new friendship, and poignant with recognition of all
that these folks had endured in recent years.

With bright, sandy beaches and lush green peaks and plains, Sierra
Leone can look like paradise. But during its civil war (1991–2002),
Sierra Leone was a living hell. It was a brutal and meaningless conflict, fed by illegal drug and diamond trading. Gangs of rebels—often
young boys who had been kidnapped, brutalized, and kept high on

drugs—sucked the life out of villages and terrorized the inhabitants, raping and maiming them, then torching their homes and moving on. After years of these horrors, a British commando invasion quickly ended the rebellion. For the next five years, a United Nations peace-keeping force occupied the country. Poorly supplied, underpaid, and undisciplined, many of the peacekeepers lived by extortion. Villagers were not sorry to see them go.

When we visited it was years after fighting had ended, but the country still struggled to recover. Freetown, the capital city on the coast, was swollen to three times its prewar population. The city had no electrical power, and the water system was danger-ously close to failure. The strain of staying alive was evident on people's faces. Up-country, where we were visiting, resilient farm-ing people were trying to rebuild their lives. They were putting food on their plates, but the schools were overcrowded and poorly supplied, burned-out modern homes and businesses often were replaced with mud-brick traditional dwellings, and a generation of teens and young adults had no ability to read or write. Kids had no shots, and many suffered from measles and malaria. The average life expectancy was about forty.

So if you were in their situation, what would you ask God to give you?

Surely God's people in Kabala pray for help all the time. They pray, fervently, for their daily rice, for rain and seed and the health and strength to raise their crop. Children fall sick and there is no medicine; parents plead with the Lord to heal them.

Yet when the pastor preached on 1 Kings 3 while we were there, his sermon in Krio (the Leonean's English-derived trade language) was entitled "Give We Sense." The pastor told his people that just as God wanted to know the desires of Solomon's heart and to grant him his deepest request, God wants to know our hearts and wants to give us what we need. The pastor said that he struggled with Sol-omon's answer. There is so much that we need, he said: a long life, some material blessings, some protection from those who would do us harm. But see what Solomon asks for: a discerning heart, the wisdom to distinguish right from wrong, for the sake of justice and good order in the land. The pastor pled with his hearers to ask God for the same thing: "Give we sense!" If we ask and receive wisdom and discernment from God, he said, then God promises that the rest will follow.

So in a land where the task of rebuilding is so immense, and the daily struggle to make it is so challenging, here were Christian brothers and sisters, some of whom could not read and write, asking for wisdom and discernment. This was wisdom born, I believe, out of the experience of extreme distress, the meltdown of government, and the breakdown of social norms. People had learned, through it all, to have radical trust in God. These village people, who were trusting God's word, were coming up with wisdom that on a secular level has taken decades for Africa experts to discover.

What does Africa need? After fifty years of opinions and failed efforts, the experts are finally saying something quite basic. Africa needs wise rule—good governance, transparency, accountability, and discernment—for administering justice and promoting the common good.

Our Christian brothers and sisters in up-country Sierra Leone seemed to know these things already. And they were bold to take it upon themselves, as New Testament people of God and agents of God's reign, to ask for what the Old Testament portrays as the privilege of a king.

In an amazing coincidence, our pastor back home in Michigan preached on the same text a month later. It was a good sermon, but the focus was entirely different. It was on our individual needs and concerns, all about "my God and me." Our Leonean brothers and sisters were thinking in much more collective and communal terms: not "give *me* sense" but "give *we* sense." They know what we need to rediscover. We are in this struggle for God's reign together. We need to think, pray, and act in together terms and seek the larger good of our land.

Africa is now one of the great heartlands of world Christianity, and the people we met there are now among the world's more typical Christians. Their way of reading the Bible and discerning its message is now among the "normal" ways by which God's word comes to believers today. That can be a tough thing for northern Christians to acknowledge. We are not at or near the center of God's work in the world today. Much more rapidly than many of us proud northern Christians can accept, we are encountering a powerful and authoritative witness from the global South church. I can't help but think now, in a season of much political nonsense here in the United States, that we would do well to pray for wise rule.

REFLECTION AND DISCUSSION
1. What do you ask God to give you?
2. How would your life as a believer change if you responded to God more in terms of "we" rather than "me"?

FURTHER STUDY
Learn more about Christianity in West Africa by reading Lamin Sanneh's *West African Christianity: The Religious Impact*. Ishmael Beah's *A Long Way Gone: Memoirs of a Boy Soldier* gives a firsthand account of the Leonean civil war's deep cruelty and how he began the road to recovery.

PRAYER
Lord, give we sense.

I Am Doing a Great Work and
I Cannot Come Down

Nehemiah 6:1-15

Andrea L. Turpin

> Sanballat and Geshem sent to me, saying, "Come and let us meet
> together in one of the villages in the plain of Ono." But they
> intended to do me harm. So I sent messengers to them, saying, "I
> am doing a great work and I cannot come down. Why should the
> work stop while I leave it to come down to you?"
>
> (Neh. 6:2-3)

In the spring of 2009 I visited the grave of Mary Lyon (1797–1849)
on the campus of Mount Holyoke College. I wanted to place a flower
on it, but I could not for the life of me find a flower store close to
campus. I briefly toyed with the idea of surreptitiously clipping one
on campus but then decided that since Lyon founded the college,
those were already "her" flowers. In the end, I decided that I should
be the flower on her grave through how I lived my life.

Who was Mary Lyon and why did she inspire that sort of devotion, so many years later, from a historian like me? Mary Lyon grew
up in rural New England during the early American republic. She
mastered and valued the domestic arts that constituted the focus of

many American women of her era, yet she simultaneously enjoyed an incredibly active mind and proved a voracious learner at school.

As a teenager Lyon experienced conversion to personal faith in Christ as Lord and Savior. After entrusting her life to Jesus, she never married or had children. Instead, Lyon channeled her considerable talents toward reproducing in another way: she educated women. Lyon facilitated the conversion of hundreds of young women and the full development of their God-given minds. She then trained these women to be teachers who would go and do likewise with their students.

Women at the time could not be pastors, but Lyon realized they could make disciples widely this way instead. Lyon creatively stewarded the particular talents God had given her within the particular situation in which she found herself.

No collegiate education for women existed in the early 1800s, but women's education between the high school and junior college levels was expanding. These schools were interchangeably known as "academies" or "seminaries." Lyon got the best education available to her, and then proceeded in 1837 to found an even better school: Mount Holyoke Female Seminary, the first permanently endowed women's higher educational institution. It wasn't quite college level during Lyon's lifetime, but she continued to raise standards and it eventually reached that mark.

She hoped to equip her students to share the gospel by serving as missionary-minded teachers in their hometowns, the American West, and abroad. She was wildly successful. Fifty years after the school's founding, a significant majority of its students had served as Christian teachers, with 178 serving as foreign missionaries.

Lyon was animated by an educational outlook I call "evangelical pragmatism," which is the desire to educate as many people as possible, as cheaply as possible, and to communicate the Christian message as well as possible. In service to the main goal of spreading the gospel, Lyon was willing to ignore some cultural norms, including those dictating women's behavior.

Some of the gender norms Mary Lyon ignored were traveling unaccompanied and speaking freely with strangers during the journey. Lyon did both in order to raise money for Mount Holyoke. When criticized for this behavior, she quoted Nehemiah's response to his detractors when he was rebuilding the wall of Jerusalem: "I am doing a great work. I cannot come down."

At the same time, Lyon embraced and used women's culture in the service of Christ. She wanted to make excellent higher education available to as many women as possible, including poor ones. So she had Mount Holyoke students do all of the institution's cooking and cleaning. No domestic servants had to be hired, which drove down the cost. This solution could not have been used to make men's higher education more affordable—men at the time were not raised with the requisite skills.

Lyon used the skills her female students took pride in, along with their sense of feminine identity as nurturers of the next generation, and taught these women how to use that combination to spread the Christian message as widely as possible. Not only did Lyon's students provide education and gospel knowledge to children in America and abroad, but many also trained other female teachers by founding schools patterned after their alma mater.

As a fellow Christian woman teacher, I admire how Lyon used all those identities to serve God. She valued the types of work historically performed by women and the bonds women forged around that work. At the same time, she did not fall victim to the Pharisees' trap of "rejecting the commandment of God in order to keep your tradition" (Mark 7:9). Customs of female behavior were just that—customs—and she disregarded them when they hindered the spread of the gospel.

REFLECTION AND DISCUSSION

1. What are some unique talents God has given you? What are some unique situations in which you find yourself? How might you creatively use this combination to advance the good news of Jesus Christ?

2. Can you think of any cultural expectations that are not actually Scriptural that may be holding you back from serving God in the most effective way possible?

FURTHER STUDY

A readable modern biography of Mary Lyon is Elizabeth Alden Green's *Mary Lyon and Mount Holyoke: Opening the Gates*. My own book, *A New Moral Vision*, features Lyon among other evangelical women who reshaped higher education in the nineteenth century. Another good option is an edited collection of Lyon's letters interwoven with a narrative of her life that her friend Edward Hitchcock published in 1851. This work, *The Power of Christian Benevolence Illustrated in the Life and Labors of Mary Lyon*, was intended for devotional use and is available today as a relatively inexpensive reprint.

PRAYER

Heavenly Father, grant us the wisdom to discern how we might use our talents where you have planted us to glorify your name. Grant us also the courage to disregard unscriptural limitations on our service. In Jesus' name, through the power of the Holy Spirit. Amen.

Our Dwelling Place

Psalm 90

Shirley A. Mullen

> Lord, you have been our dwelling place
>> in all generations.
> Before the mountains were brought forth,
>> or ever you had formed the earth and the world,
>> from everlasting to everlasting you are God.

(Ps. 90:1-2)

Historians, like all human beings, walk in the faint light of hopes, beliefs, and abstractions that we affirm but cannot prove. We work, not with the certainty of logical syllogisms or mathematical equations, but always in the midst of the messiness of concrete particularity. The daily realities of our work and our lives are negotiated out of this tension. We yearn to see clearly and understand fully, but the material of our craft yields only partial responses to our questions. Our discipline forces us to reckon with limitations—indeed is forged out of that limitation. Psalm 90 captures the complexities of the historian's—and any human being's—reality.

We live and work with the mysterious consciousness of eternity. All around us we see evidence that the world began before we arrived, and we are vaguely but persistently aware that it will continue when we are no longer here to enjoy it. As historians, we seek to explore and ultimately to make meaning for others out of this abstraction we call "the past." We tell stories that seem to make it more accessible, and in doing so create a context in which to locate and give deeper meaning to our present experience.

In Psalm 90, the psalmist invites us to see this haunting abstraction of eternity in personal terms. Long before Blaise Pascal articulated the human terror of being "swallowed up in the infinite immensity of spaces of which I know nothing and which know nothing of me," we had been called to consider the universe as a "dwelling place" where we are surrounded on all sides by a person—and not just any person, but the Person who has set the context and terms of our very existence.

While the universe may be personal, it is not comfortable. Against the eternity of our "dwelling place," we are fleeting and insubstantial, the stuff of dust, dreams, and sighs. As historians, we have the privileged task of seeking out and narrating the stories of these fleeting bits of dust, dreams, and sighs—whether they be individuals, communities, institutions, or civilizations—seeking to narrate their stories and thereby extending, at least for a time, their capacity for agency and impact.

The psalmist reminds us that it is not just our finitude but also our failures that make us uncomfortable in the company of the Eternal Presence. We know ourselves to be less than we want to be—than we ought to be. Nevertheless, we believe—somewhere deep inside—that we were created for more. Despite our finitude and fallenness, we believe ourselves to be responsible—to be agents, rather than victims, in our own stories.

It falls on the historian to narrate the human experience in a way that does justice to the particularities and complexities of our daily lives—to suggest meaning and purpose, but not predictability and inexorability; to show enough of our darkness so that we are not deceived, but enough of our potential so that we do not despair.

In the closing prayer, the psalmist invites us to see our lives from a perspective that invites both humility and hopefulness: "So teach us to count our days that we may gain a wise heart" (v. 12). Those words remind us once again of Pascal's warning to "realize our limitations. We are something and we are not everything." But more than that, the psalmist invites us to see our lives in a way that includes the promise of God's partnering presence. It is an invitation growing out of a certain way of seeing the world: more imagination than argument.

As historians—and as human beings—we are not required by the evidence to see pattern or providence. In the words of the Christian historian Herbert Butterfield, "It is possible to read history and study the course of centuries without seeing God in the story at all; just as it is possible for men to live their lives in the present day without seeing that God has any part to play." But he goes on to remind us that the psalmist came from a people who chose to see God as the God of History: participating in Creation, mysteriously and always on God's own terms, but in a way that allows us to live and work in a context of meaning and hope.

REFLECTION AND DISCUSSION

1. According to Herbert Butterfield, "Only those who have brought God home to themselves in this way (i.e., in their daily lives) will be able to see him in history." How do you see God in your daily life?
2. How does living with a sense of our finitude contribute to "gaining a wise heart"?

FURTHER STUDY

For further reflection on how we might live more fully from a sense of God's presence in the midst of our finitude, see Herbert Butterfield, "God in History" (from *Writings on Christianity and History*) and Dietrich Bonhoeffer, "After Ten Years: A Reckoning at New Year 1943" (from *Letters and Papers from Prison*).

PRAYER

God of Time and Eternity, may we value the opportunities of this day, knowing that you will take the very work of our hands and make it part of your eternal purposes.

The Work of Our Hands—
In Perspective

Psalm 90

Mark A. Noll

> Let your work be manifest to your servants,
> and your glorious power to their children.
> Let the favor of the Lord our God be upon us,
> and prosper for us the work of our hands—
> O prosper the work of our hands!
>
> (Ps. 90:16-17)

Isaac Watts' great hymn, which was based on Psalm 90, was originally composed to hearten English Dissenters at a time in their history when they faced accusations of treasonous disloyalty—and when the entire nation was threatened by the Jacobite invasion of 1715: "Our God, our help in ages past, / Our hope for years to come." When later editors, including John Wesley, altered "our God" to "O God," the hymn took its place as a general encouragement for all believers at all times, rather than just for a single beleaguered minority undergoing particular trials at a particular time.

Historians in our day might follow Isaac Watts in thinking that this psalm spoke particularly to them, while at the same time recognizing with Watts' editors that its message cannot be restricted to only themselves. Yet for historians there is much to ponder.

The psalm's utter realism about the transitory character of all existence should sober those of us who study the past. However wide-ranging our reading and research, however painstaking our scholarly writing, however patient we are with our students, our labors have the permanence of "dust" (v. 3). If we are realistic about our individual accomplishments and the achievements of our institutions, we must acknowledge that they partake fully in the "toil and trouble" of ordinary life; whatever their positive value, they "are soon gone and fly away" (v. 10).

The eighth verse of this psalm should give special pause to historians: "You have set our iniquities before you, our secret sins in the light of your countenance." I am confident that as academics, students, and teachers, much of our work does spring from good intentions, that the motives getting us up each morning are often altruistic, unselfish, kind, and other-centered. Yet the psalm offers a stark reminder that the Lord knows our "secret sins"—our heedless obsessions about our own projects, our inability to forget slights whether real or imagined, our instinct to believe that it really is about us, our schadenfreude at our colleagues' difficulties, our envy of those at better institutions or with brighter reputations, and, above all, our pride. Even if, as a tribe, historians enjoy a better than average reputation as disciplined, curious, helpful, and (not incidentally) good candidates for administrative leadership, the psalm is a reminder that standing in the eyes of the world is not the same as standing before God.

Yet as so often happens in Scripture, realism about the human condition gives way to realism about divine mercy. With expectation of a positive answer, the psalmist asks the Lord to "turn," to "have compassion," and to "make us glad as many days as you have afflicted us" (vv. 13-15). Because God's work can be "manifest in your servants, and your glorious power in your children" (v. 16), life can in fact be much more than a tale told by an idiot, full of sound and fury, meaning nothing. Instead, with words that are particularly relevant for those who slog away day by day in the classroom, the office, the library, and on websites, the psalmist asserts that our work is worthy of "the favor of the Lord God among us." Such reassurance makes for a fitting return and the tempered hope with which Isaac Watts ended his enduring hymn: "Be thou our guard while troubles last, / And our eternal home."

REFLECTION AND DISCUSSION

1. Is it actually possible to be as humble about our doings as verses 3-11 require and at the same time as optimistic as verses 11-13 allow?
2. The pivot of Psalm 90 is verse 12: "So teach us to count our days that we may gain a wise heart." What might living with a "wise heart" look like in your life?

FURTHER STUDY

An excellent article that includes treatment of Isaac Watts' hymn as written especially for English Dissenters in the 1710s is Rochelle A. Stackhouse, "Hymnody and Politics: Isaac Watts's 'Our God, Our Help in Ages Past' and Timothy Dwight's 'I Love Thy Kingdom Lord,'" in *Wonderful Words of Life: Hymns in American Protestant History and Theology*, ed. Richard J. Mouw and Mark A. Noll. A history of the hymn, including the work of editors like John Wesley, is well described in John Julian, *A Dictionary of Hymnology* (1957).

PRAYER

Lord, you have been our dwelling place in all generations. Yet the days of *our life*, which soon pass away, are only toil and trouble. Turn, we pray, and have compassion on your servants. Make us glad for as many years as we have seen evil. Let your favor be upon us, and prosper the work of our hands—O prosper the work of our hands.

Celebrating Failure

Psalm 120

Shivraj K. Mahendra

> Too long have I had my dwelling
>   among those who hate peace.
> I am for peace;
>   but when I speak,
>   they are for war.

(Ps. 120:6-7)

History is a narrative of success and failure and everything in between. While the world in general celebrates only success, Christianity goes beyond. Christians have the confidence to celebrate even failure because they know that failure, loss, or even demise do not have the final word. Eternal God has the final word. That final word is resurrection, the great restoration of everything in Christ.

But within history, the experience of failure is real and painful. In our own Christian journey, we can recollect our failures; some of us may still be recovering from their depressing impacts. In the context of global Christian ministry, the sense of failure may be especially felt with regard to world peace.

A noteworthy example is that of E. Stanley Jones, a Methodist missionary and statesman in the twentieth century. In his autobiography, *A Song of Ascents*, Jones outlines several of his failed attempts at contributing to world peace. First, the failure to stop the war between the United States and Japan. He negotiated between the governments so that the Pearl Harbor tragedy could be avoided. Then a few years later, he mediated between Muslim and Hindu leaders so that an independent India would not have to be divided into two nations: Pakistan and India. Unfortunately, all his attempts failed. Both tragedies cost thousands of lives.

Jones' experience points to the agony of the great psalmist David. A man after God's own heart, David took no delight in violent conflict. But he was surrounded by people who wanted something else. "I am for peace," David lamented, "but when I speak, they are for war."

Today we, too, are surrounded by people waging different types of war, some in the name of religion. Christians are being persecuted and slaughtered for their faith. How do we work for peace in the violent contexts of our times? What if we fail?

Reflecting on his failures, E. Stanley Jones wrote, "It is not ours to succeed or fail—it is ours to do the highest we know and leave results with God. For he has a way of rescuing some good out of apparent failure." God can turn our mourning into dancing. Success and victory belong to him. May the Lord help us to trust in him and be his instruments of peace in all that we do.

REFLECTION AND DISCUSSION
1. Have you ever failed in your life? What is it like to fail?
2. How would you succeed? What do you expect from God? What do you hope from yourself?

FURTHER STUDY
E. Stanley Jones' autobiography, *A Song of Ascents*, was published in 1968 and remains in print. On failure, see also J. R. Briggs, *Fail: Finding Hope and Grace in the Midst of Ministry Failure*. Michael Long's *Christian Peace and Nonviolence* is a documentary history of that complicated topic.

PRAYER

God of peace and success, please grant me the grace to do my best even in times of failure. Save me from loss of trust and empower me to remain energetic and optimistic in all that I do for your glory. Help me to celebrate failure with confidence in your resurrection power. In Jesus' name, Amen.

Learning to Lament

Psalm 137

Trisha Posey

> By the rivers of Babylon, there we sat down, Yea! we wept when we remembered Zion. We hanged our harps upon the willows in the midst thereof. For there they that carried us away captive required of us a song; and they that wasted us required of us mirth, saying, Sing us one of the songs of Zion.
>
> (Ps. 137:1-3, KJV)

On July 5, 1852 the runaway slave and abolitionist speaker Frederick Douglass delivered one of the most famous speeches in American history. At the heart of his speech was the question, "What to the slave is the Fourth of July?" His answer to his white audience: "a day that reveals to him, more than all other days in the year, the gross injustice and cruelty to which he is the constant victim."

Douglass found it ironic that he had been called upon by his white audience to speak about a holiday celebrating American freedoms while millions of enslaved men and women remained in bondage. Even while he recounted the triumph of liberal ideals in the American Revolution, he was compelled to view the Fourth of July from the perspective of those held in bondage, those whose song was not one of freedom but of captivity and torment. Calling upon Scripture, Douglass then entered into a spirit of lament. "I can to-day take up the plaintive lament of a peeled and woe-smitten people!" he exclaimed, then quoted the lines above from the King James translation of Psalm 137.

Douglass could have found multiple examples of lament in Scripture from which to draw, including many other psalms, the words of many Old Testament prophets, and especially the Book of Lamentations. Lament is a biblical action, one that recognizes both the reality of the fallenness of this world and God's care for his suffering people in the midst of that reality. In his book *Dark Clouds, Deep Mercy*, Mark Vroegop describes lament as "a prayer in pain that leads to trust." As Vroegop explains it, lament includes four key elements: an address to God, a complaint, a request, and an expression of trust and/or praise.

This pattern would have been deeply familiar to Frederick Douglass and other enslaved persons in the nineteenth century, who lived out a pain that was similar to the captive Israelites. Their lament was a grief rooted in slavery, alienation, and bitter separation from loved ones. Douglass eloquently voiced his dismay with the egregious state of affairs in the slave-holding United States. Yet, as with the psalmists, Douglass did not present his grievance without hope. Instead, he concluded his complaint with a request to God penned by fellow abolitionist William Lloyd Garrison:

> God speed the year of Jubilee
> The wide world o'er!
> When from their galling chains set free,
> Th' oppress'd shall vilely bend the knee,
> And wear the yoke of tyranny
> Like brutes no more.

Like Garrison, Douglass fully trusted that God would restore "freedom's reign" and "to man his plundered rights."

Reading Douglass, who knew and practiced the pattern of lament in a very public way, always reminds me of the importance of lament for myself and my community, particularly in our consideration of the past. No one can engage in the study of history without encountering difficult, sometimes inexplicable, situations of pain, suffering, and evil. Instead of offering trite answers to such suffering, sometimes the only response can be one of lament.

For Christians who live in the United States, it can sometimes be tempting to highlight the triumphs of American history and tie those successes to a belief that God has uniquely blessed the United States. But Christians, as Douglass reminded us, are also called upon to recognize and lament the failures of the nation.

As Soong-Chan Rah notes, "To only have a theology of celebration at the cost of the theology of suffering is incomplete." In the spirit of Frederick Douglass, may our understanding of the gospel and its work in history embrace both celebration and suffering.

REFLECTION AND DISCUSSION

1. What are some areas of the past that you need to revisit in a spirit of lament?
2. How can you practice lament more regularly in your church and your community?

FURTHER STUDY

For more on Douglass, read the new biography by David Blight, *Frederick Douglass: Prophet of Freedom*. You can learn more about the theology of lament in Soong-Chan Rah's *Prophetic Lament: A Call for Justice in Troubled Times* and Mark Vroegop's *Dark Clouds, Deep Mercy: Discovering the Grace of Lament*.

PRAYER

Our heavenly Father, thank you that you invite us through your Scripture to lament the brokenness that we see in the world. As we learn more about that brokenness through our study of the past, help us to mourn with those who have mourned and to be drawn in faith to you, recognizing that in our lament we can trust that you will respond to our calls for justice because you are a just God.

Who Is a Woman of Valor?

Proverbs 31

Nadya Williams

> Charm is deceitful, and beauty is vain,
>   but a woman who fears the LORD is to be praised.
> Give her a share in the fruit of her hands,
>   and let her works praise her in the city gates.
>
> (Prov. 31:30-31)

For the past half a millennium, the ushering in of Shabbat in many an observant Jewish home has included the recitation of the hymn "Eshet Chayil" ("Woman of Valor"). In this context, Proverbs 31:10-31 continues to provide a link between the Old Testament women of valor—from Sarah to Bathsheba—and the more modern wife whose family recites the passage in her honor. Considering how much work Jewish women have traditionally had to put into the preparation of the home—especially meals for Shabbat—the outpouring of gratitude for the woman of the house each Friday evening is certainly apt! Furthermore, through this weekly repetition of Proverbs 31, the past seamlessly connects to the present in traditional Jewish homes, inserting each Jewish wife into the lineage of worthy biblical women.

But for Christian women, Proverbs 31 has not had the same sweet association. Rather, it has elicited a sense of dread, as so many feel inadequate and unable ever to live up to its description of the ideal woman.

My personal connection with the passage stems from the way in which it allows so many aspects of my own life to collide. I grew up in a secular Jewish home in Russia and Israel, then came to Christ as an adult. Through both my growing-up years and now as a classicist and ancient historian, I continue to be fascinated by the culture and society of the Ancient Mediterranean. Last but not least, I am a wife and mother. I read Proverbs 31 through all these lenses at once.

The laudatory portrayal of the wife in this passage is striking for me as an ancient historian, because the view that it presents is utterly countercultural and unique in the context of the Ancient Mediterranean. While the Jews respected women as made in the image of God, just as men were, their neighbors throughout the Mediterranean and the Ancient Near East believed women were created as a punishment and a curse for men. Indeed, the first woman created in Greek mythology, Pandora, was the gods' cursed gift to Epimetheus, intended to punish humanity for his brother Prometheus' attempts to steal fire from Zeus. In the sixth century B.C., the poet Semonides listed ten different types of wives, largely basing them on the mare, the dog, the donkey, and other unflattering animals. Only one of the ten, the bumblebee, is good. Semonides makes it clear, however, that the odds of finding this rare, good wife are not in any man's favor.

I see Proverbs 31 as the ancient Jews' response, inspired by God, to the culture of the Gentiles around them. Whereas their neighbors saw women (and wives) as a necessary curse, the Jews saw them as a blessing to all mankind, from Adam forth. Proverbs 31 is organized, as a result, in concentric circles of influence of the good wife. She sees the needs of others, and her purposeful works and attention bless all, beginning with her husband and children and radiating outward to the entire community.

Wouldn't it be wonderful for Christian women to reclaim this traditional Jewish reading of this passage? For me, as a wife and mother, such a reading has an encouraging application, as it allows me to view all of my work, both in the home and in my career, as blessing others—from my husband and children to colleagues, friends, students, etc. And for men reading this passage, let its last two verses serve as encouragement to openly acknowledge the contributions of the women in their lives and, through that praise, bless their works.

Yet the Jewish reading of the passage is not complete if we do not connect it to Christ. The wife in this passage is the ultimate embodiment of Jesus' command to love one's neighbor. Ultimately, Christian women are right to fear the Proverbs 31 wife as too perfect and unattainable a model—for it is the church, washed by the blood of Jesus, who is the perfect redeemed bride of the King.

REFLECTION AND DISCUSSION

1. How have you seen and interpreted the Proverbs 31 wife in the past? What strikes you as encouraging about this hymn? Have you ever found it to be discouraging?
2. In what ways could we benefit from seeing the perfect wife as referring to the church as Jesus' bride?

FURTHER STUDY

The fragment of Semonides is quite shocking and well worth reading for its contrast with Proverbs 31 (www.stoa.org/diotima/anthology/sem_7.shtml). For a history of the place of that Scripture in the Jewish Shabbat ritual, read Yehuda Sherpin's "Why Sing Eishet Chayil on Friday Night?" at www.chabad.org. Finally, Rachel Held Evans' blog post on Proverbs 31 expresses the typical frustration of many Christian women with the passage, and provides a thoughtful analysis of it (rachelheldevans.com/blog/3-things-you-might-not-know -about-proverbs-31).

PRAYER

Lord, make me a blessing to others! Bring this Scripture to my mind, and let it shine in encouragement on those nights when my lamp indeed is not going out, as the baby is up at 2am, or other needs and obligations consume my mind and time. May these busy and often exhausting seasons bless others and be for your glory! Amen.

The Call to Work in Faith

Ecclesiastes 9:7-10

Jonathan Den Hartog

> Whatever your hand finds to do, do with your might.
> (Eccl. 9:10a)

How do you think about your work? Is it simply a job, a way to pay the bills and put food on the table? Is it a way to employ your time, whether in a nine to five capacity or through a series of gigs? Is it a path to self-fulfillment and the definition of who you are, your identity? A deeper and richer understanding of our work can be found in the Christian understanding of vocation.

Coming from the Latin word meaning "to call," vocation envisions God giving each believer a twofold call. The first is a call to himself, to believe in faith—a general calling. The second is a call to serve in a specific place that will do good for others and thereby build up the Kingdom—a specific calling. In seeking to appreciate the richness of the doctrine of vocation, there is much that can be learned from the Puritans.

The Puritans were zealous English Christians in the era of the Protestant Reformation, with their flourishing from the 1550s to 1640s. One branch even migrated to the New World in the 1630s, where they set up colonies in New England—especially Massachusetts Bay. On both sides of the Atlantic Ocean, these Puritans sought to "purify" the Church of England and thereby extend the work of the Reformation. By returning to the Scriptures, they believed the Church would be more fully reformed. Their passion for reform was not only for the corporate church; it extended to the reform of individual lives as well. They thus called ordinary people to take up their callings with passion and purpose.

Among the immigrants to New England, one well-known Puritan minister was John Cotton. In England he had pastored a church in Boston, Lincolnshire named St. Botolph's, but in 1633 his path brought him to the new Boston recently founded in New England. Established as a pastor, Cotton was noted for the way he combined systematic theology with heartfelt preaching. His sermons were eagerly attended, and many reported coming to faith through them.

Cotton also applied the Scripture to many areas of life—including vocation. His sermon on "Christian Calling" is a powerful communication of his Puritan, Christian view of work.

Cotton sets his entire discussion of Christian vocation in the context of faith. Because the Christian is saved by faith, he or she also desires to work by faith. Work, according to Cotton, should serve both others and the common good: "We live by faith in our vocations, in that faith, in serving God, serves men, and in serving men, serves God." Faithful work, no matter what the position, is meant to serve. Once placed in a calling, the believer looks to God by faith for help in that calling: "Faith saith not, 'give me such a calling and turn me loose to it;' but faith looks up to heaven for skill and ability."

Faith motivates specific actions within work. Cotton says that faith propels the believer to face "the most homeliest [common or menial], and difficultest and most dangerous things." Faith propels work to take on challenges but banishes pride as if some part of the job were below the believer. Christians show humility in service and thereby model Christ, who washed his disciples' feet. Next, faith trusts God with the burdens of work: "[F]aith casts all the failings and burdens of his calling upon the Lord; that is the proper work of faith; it rolls and casts all upon Him." Thus, faith trusts God in the middle of the work and shows itself to be faithful by yielding all cares to him. Cotton identifies troubles that might come in the middle of the work—cares about the success of the work, fears about the work, and even the dangers that might come from the work. All are to be entrusted to God's care.

To Cotton, the final act of faith expressed through work is to lay down that very calling. When human circumstance, divine direction, or even illness and death direct that a vocation is to be laid down, faith relinquishes it in trust. The Christian in his or her work can lay it down "with comfort and boldness in the sight of God and man." If the work has been done in faith, then it can also be given up in faith.

Now, the community of Boston to which Cotton preached this sermon came to be distinguished for its hard work. When properly understood, what's often called the "Protestant Work Ethic" was an outgrowth of zealous faith. If, in later years, that energy degenerated merely into productive capitalism, it should not overshadow Cotton's clear, biblical account of how faith can work its way out in vocations.

REFLECTION AND DISCUSSION

1. How do you think about your work? Is it a calling? Is it a place where you can live out your faith?
2. What challenges are you confronting in your work right now? How are they opportunities to practice faith?

FURTHER STUDY

John Cotton's complete sermon can be found in the volume *The American Puritans: Their Prose and Poetry*, edited by Perry Miller. If you'd like to read a nice introduction to the Puritans and their practical lives, check out Leland Ryken's *Worldly Saints: The Puritans as They Really Were*. For a broader overview of the Puritan movement, consider delving into Michael Winship's *Hot Protestants: A History of Puritanism in England and America*.

PRAYER

O God, you are the one who calls us to yourself. You also call us to places of work and service. But the connection between your calling and our callings is not always an easy one, and it is often complicated by the broken world in which we live. So, we pray today for those who are seeking to discern your calling for them—young people and those looking to change employment—give them wisdom to follow you by faith. We pray for those who sense a call but lack a path to it, those desiring to follow a path but who have their way blocked, for the unemployed and underemployed. Give them hope to continue to walk in the way you are leading. We pray for those in vocations, that you will grant them faith to serve well as they trust in you. Give them courage to meet the challenges that interfere with their calling. Finally, we pray for those who are being called to lay down a vocation, because of retirement, health issues, or career moves. Grant them faith to trust you both with the work that has been done and in the callings you still have for them. Take all of our labor up into your Kingdom. And we pray this in the name of Jesus, the one who fulfilled the callings on his life perfectly. Amen.

The God Who Restores

Isaiah 25:1-9

Mary R. S. Bracy

> For you have been a refuge to the poor,
>   a refuge to the needy in their distress . . .
>   he will swallow up death forever.
> Then the Lord GOD will wipe away the tears from all faces,
> and the disgrace of his people he will take away from all the
> earth, for the LORD has spoken.
>
> (Isa. 25:4a, 8)

On April 19, 1995, I was eight years old and riding in the back seat of my mother's car when a breaking news bulletin came on the radio: a bomb had gone off at the federal building in Oklahoma City, about thirty miles from where we lived. I was too young to really understand what had happened, but I knew that it was something bad. It was a disaster and act of terror that changed everything about the place where I grew up.

The question of why bad things happen is hard for anyone, and it's especially hard for Christians. The bad things that we don't understand keep happening, and they seem overwhelming. Reports of terrorism, ethnic cleansing, and natural disasters fill the airwaves. Closer to home, we see things that cause us and our loved ones pain. Divorce. Cancer. Heartbreak. Loss. All of these things can cause us to bury our heads in our hands and ask God: "Why? How could you let this happen?"

Speaking at a memorial service in Oklahoma City just days after the bombing, the Rev. Billy Graham gave voice to these questions:

> I've been asked why God allows it. I don't know. I can't give a direct answer. I have to confess that I never fully understand—even for my own satisfaction. I have to accept by faith that God is a God of love and mercy and compassion—even in the midst of suffering. . . . The Bible says God is not the author of evil. And it speaks of evil in 1 Thessalonians as a mystery. There's something about evil that we will never understand this side of eternity.

Graham then pointed to something else that Christians know to be true: God is the God of restoration. "Yes, there is hope," Graham said. "There's hope for the present because I believe that the stage is already being set for the restoration and renewal of the spirit of this city."

For the people of Oklahoma City, this message fell on open ears. As families grieved their loved ones, the city grieved with them. And slowly, after the dust had settled and the rubble was cleared, restoration and renewal slowly took shape. The city built a memorial, with a field of 168 empty chairs, one for each life lost. A yearly marathon took runners through the streets of Oklahoma City, past flags printed with the names of bombing victims. Over the years, the city incorporated the bombing into its identity. It was an incredible tragedy. But in the midst of it, the city came together. The evil could not be understood. But the restoration happened anyway.

Six years later, on September 11, 2001, I stood in a high school classroom watching as images of terror and destruction once again came over the television. In the days after, trying to find a way to express the jumbled emotions of fear, anger, and unspeakable grief, my church choir director pulled out an anthem written in the aftermath of the Oklahoma City bombing and dedicated to the people of that city. And we lifted our voices, trying once again to find comfort in a God of restoration:

Lord, you are God, ruling in gentleness.
Lord, you are God. You wipe away each tear.
You hear our every prayer.
You give us comfort.
You touch our hearts and calm our fears.
You are eternal! Alpha, Omega!
We place our hope in you alone.
You are the God who restores.

The restoration comes. It comes slowly, at God's pace and not at our own. It comes haltingly. It comes in nights of tears and anger and questioning why and how something like this could possibly happen. *But it comes.* God is the God who restores.

REFLECTION AND DISCUSSION
1. What in your life is in need of God's restoration?
2. Where have you seen God's restoration in the past?

FURTHER READING
The choral anthem quoted here is Joseph M. Martin's "Canticle of Hope." You can find recordings of it on YouTube. If you want to learn more about how Oklahoma City recovered from the bombing, visit https://memorialmuseum.com.

PRAYER
Almighty God, we know that you can bring restoration to even the most painful of situations. Lord, I turn to you and cry out in hope. I pray that you would bring restoration where there has been destruction, comfort where there has been pain, and peace where there has been grief. In the name of Jesus, Amen.

Before You Were Conceived

Jeremiah 1:4-10

Verónica A. Gutiérrez

> Before I formed you in the womb I knew you; and before
> you were born I consecrated you; I appointed you a prophet
> to the nations.
>
> (Jer. 1:5)

When I was a girl, someone gifted me a small, laminated inspirational name card. It may have been my mother. Olive green in color with "Veronica" printed in cursive across the top, the second parenthetical line (Latin Origin) was followed by a third: "True Image." The opening verses of Jeremiah 1:5 appeared below, with the faint imprint of a tawny sparrow perched on a branch visible in the background. Many years and many moves later, I now display that cherished little name card in my faculty office. My name's significance and the accompanying Scripture (albeit with a missing line) remind me that I nearly died of a bacterial infection when I was 11 months old; my recovery after 41 days in the hospital baffled doctors, but not my mother. A devout Catholic, she gave me this card, I believe, to remind me of my miraculous second chance, and to encourage me to live my life for the Lord, in whose true image (*vera icon*) I was created and consecrated before conception. Classically educated amongst similarly minded Catholic families, and emboldened by my parents' encouragement and example, as a youth I felt well-equipped to live for the Lord. Unlike Jeremiah, who referenced his youth as a handicap, I relished my childhood. How could it be difficult to live for the Lord if everyone around you was doing the same? My youth harbored me from the world.

Curiosity about my family's faith prompted me to study the origins of Mexican Catholicism, and I eventually settled on a career as a colonial Mexican historian. During my doctoral studies I lived in Mexico for a year visiting archives, learning Nahuatl (Aztec), finessing my Spanish, and participating in various ritualistic expressions of my ancestral Catholicism. I had found a way to live my faith through my work. Within the secular environments in which I trained, the centrality of my faith was well-known; if not always shared, it was respected.

Then, like Jeremiah, I faltered. In the fall of 2012, I stepped into a classroom for my first lecture on my first day at an evangelical Christian institution, a community with whom I had limited exposure. My World History course became heated as students began quoting Scripture and verse at each other during a discussion of our human origins. All my knowledge of Patristics and theology had not equipped me to respond in kind. Concerned that students might question my Christianity or lose respect for me before I had earned it, I, who had been boldly Catholic all of my life, carefully crafted my responses to hide my faith. After class I phoned my fiancé (now my husband) to wonder if this was the right place for me.

Fortunately, this scenario has never repeated itself. Indeed, when I finally revealed my Catholicism in that World History class, it was a nonissue. What I learned from the experience was a deeper empathy for students who silence themselves in class, afraid to dissent or offer a competing perspective. Mostly it taught me the value of being authentic. Describing my lived experiences with Catholicism in Mexico and admitting my struggles with aspects of the Christianization project—despite being a product of that enterprise—have prompted rich discussions in my Latin American history courses. My work is itself a search for authentic voices, for my focus on indigenous participation in the evangelization process allows colonial Mexican native peoples, too often silenced, to describe their encounters with the divine. Like Jeremiah, I feel as if the Lord has touched my mouth and given me the words to speak (1:9), not to pluck down or destroy, but to unite more fully with my fellow Christ followers. This is no better exemplified than by my institutional affiliation leading me to the Conference on Faith and History, where I have been warmly embraced.

The lines from Jeremiah on the name card I received three decades ago have now come to hold a new meaning for me: twelve days before I received an invitation to write this essay, I lost my unborn child; like my hospital stay 41 years ago, she survived 41 days in my womb. In the morning, my 6-year-old daughter lost her first tooth, and in the evening, as my husband put her little brothers to bed, she sat with me, wiping away my tears as I lost her baby sister. We named our little one Ana Verónica, the hispanized inverse of my name (Verónica Anne): what my Mexican friends used to call me, and what for a decade I had longed to name a daughter. United as *true images*, there is a piece of me in heaven now. In my grief, I have returned to those words in Jeremiah, reminding myself that *before she was conceived, God knew her; though she did not come to birth, God consecrated her.* Her voice silenced, she has gone to live *with* the Lord; with my voice, I will continue to live *for* the Lord.

REFLECTION AND DISCUSSION

1. When have you found yourself feeling like an outsider, afraid to speak of the Lord with others, even those with similar beliefs? How have you overcome your fear to speak with joy of the Lord, within your church community or out in the world?

2. How can you recognize fear in others? In what ways can you encourage those afraid to speak for the Lord to use their own voice?

FURTHER STUDY

To learn more about how native people in colonial Mexico participated in their own Christianization and encountered the divine, see Jonathan Truitt's *Sustaining the Divine in Mexico Tenochtitlan: Nahuas and Catholicism, 1523–1700.*

PRAYER

Lord, you who touched the lips of Jeremiah and gave him the words to speak, give us a voice to praise you and to love you. Help us recognize fear in others and give us the wisdom to ameliorate it. Grant us the ability to be unafraid to live for you wherever we may be, whether with our words or in silent example. In Christ's name. Amen.

Our Best Teacher

Joel 2:28-32

Brenda Thompson Schoolfield

> I will pour out my Spirit on all flesh: your sons and your
> daughters shall prophesy, your old men shall dream dreams, and
> your young men shall see visions.
>
> (Joel 2:28, ESV)

Lifelong learning is one goal I have for my students. I want them to
cultivate their curiosity about this world and about other people.
This kind of learning is more self-directed than teacher-directed,
and I strive to teach my students how they can continue to learn outside class and without supervision. The Christian life—the process
of sanctification—requires continual learning in order to become
conformed to the image of Christ. "Be transformed," Paul encouraged the Romans, "by the renewal of your mind" (Rom. 12:2, ESV).
Peter challenged his readers to "supplement your faith with virtue,
and virtue with knowledge, and knowledge with self-control" so
that they would "grow in the grace and knowledge of our Lord and
Savior Jesus Christ" (2 Pet. 1:5-6; 3:18, ESV).

An honest appraisal of our abilities to pursue this spiritual lifelong learning shows us that we need direction, and Jesus promised
to send that Helper, the Holy Spirit, to his disciples. He told them,

"It is to your advantage that I go away"—Did the disciples gasp at this statement?—"for if I do not go away, the Helper will not come to you" (John 16:7, ESV). How, they may have thought, could they be better off *without* their Rabbi, their Teacher, their Lord? He was the master teacher; his use of examples, stories, and questions provide us with the exemplar of teaching. Who could possibly do better?

Jesus was telling them that the coming Helper would fulfill the promise prophesied centuries before: "I will pour out my Spirit on all flesh" (Joel 2:28, ESV). Old Testament scholars have a few different views about where and how the Holy Spirit worked before his coming at Pentecost in the first century A.D., but many of them agree that the Spirit did not indwell all those who believed in Jehovah. The Holy Spirit came, rather, to individuals such as Joshua, Gideon, or David to empower them for special tasks, or it came to prophets to give them the word of the Lord. Joel's promise of the pouring out of the Spirit to everyone comes in the middle of several promises to the children of Zion of healing, land, food, and rest.

Pentecost, known by the Jews of the first century as the Feast of the Harvest or the Feast of Weeks, celebrates the beginning of the wheat harvest. How appropriate that the Holy Spirit should come to the believers at harvest time to teach them about and empower them for the work of gathering together the members of the body for whom Christ died. The Holy Spirit makes the spiritual harvest possible.

On this journey to grow in grace, we have the best teacher to guide us into truth, goodness, and beauty. We do not have to travel, pay tuition, or set aside our work to study with him. While human teachers here on earth are temporary, the Holy Spirit is with us always. He is with every one of us, for God has called every one of his people to do his work. Joel's promise is to "all flesh" and for "your sons and your daughters." Peter recognized that promise fulfilled at Pentecost, quoting Joel's prophecy in his sermon that day (Acts 2:17-21), and he opened his first letter acknowledging the work of the Spirit in sanctification (1 Pet. 1:2). The Holy Spirit comforts, heals, leads, and empowers. God is with us still.

REFLECTION AND DISCUSSION

1. What does Spirit-filled living look like in your daily experience?
2. What life lessons are you facing today? What promise about the Holy Spirit can you claim for yourself?

FURTHER STUDY

Francis Chan and Danae Yankoski, *Forgotten God: Reversing Our Tragic Neglect of the Holy Spirit*, along with Michael Reeves, *Delighting in the Trinity*, have helped me in my own study of the Holy Spirit. Andrew Murray's classic and accessible *Experiencing the Holy Spirit* was republished in 2015.

PRAYER

Empowering God, you gave the church the abiding presence of your Holy Spirit. Look upon your church today and hear our petitions. Grant that, gathered and directed by your Spirit, we may confess Christ as Lord and combine our diverse gifts with a singular passion to continue his mission in this world until we join in your eternal praise. Amen.

"Just As You Have Said"

Amos 5:10-15

David McFarland

> Seek good and not evil,
> that you may live;
> and so the LORD, the God of hosts, will be with you,
> just as you have said.
>
> (Amos 5:14)

A recent addition to the Canadian school calendar is "Orange Shirt Day," a grassroots awareness campaign for the victims and survivors of a dark chapter in my country's past: the impact of Indian Residential Schools on Canada's indigenous peoples. As part of last year's assembly to mark the occasion, a parent in my Christian high school community shared from her experience as the daughter of residential school survivors. She spoke of her recent first visit to Ottawa, of standing in front of the national Parliament Buildings, and of being brought to tears as she considered all that had been legislated against her family and Native culture from within its chambers.

I was convicted by her vulnerable presentation and my own privileged ignorance as a non-indigenous Canadian. Even as I knew something of the residential school system (even attempting its inclusion in my history teaching), my own sentiment whenever I've stood in that same spot in front of Parliament has really only ever been gratitude for all the good things Canada affords me and offers to the world. What had my nice Canadian patriotism missed?

While I'm no Christian nationalist and I do not resent that a culturally dominant Christianity has long receded from Canadian public life, the religious and specifically Christian overtones in Canada's past are difficult to ignore. Canada sanctioned its Indian Residential School System in various forms from the mid-nineteenth century, peaking in the mid-twentieth century, until the 1990s, with the aim of "killing the Indian in the child" as a frontline effort in the settler-colonial quest for civilizational progress. This was seen as "good Christian work," a joint venture between church and state (more precisely, state *via* church) with almost all Christian denominations in Canada involved to varying degrees. The advancement of God's kingdom and national destiny were synonymous to the well-meaning, yet culturally blinded, architects of this project.

There was a dark underbelly to this "just cause," in the widespread physical, emotional, and sexual abuse of children and teenagers forcibly removed from their families and communities. All of this was recently brought to light through the Truth and Reconciliation Commission (2008–2015), modeled after the post-Apartheid reckoning in South Africa. It is encouraging and important justice work that many Canadian churches have joined in this ongoing national healing.

Immediately prior to articulating the well-known biblical vision where justice would "roll down like waters" (5:24), the Hebrew prophet Amos calls out the gap between the rhetoric and reality of divine presence among those who invoke God's name. Only where there is justice will the claim "God is with us" be true.

The implication is that there are those who, consciously or not, misspeak for and of God. I hear echoes of this in Christ's own injunction: "many will say to me, 'Lord, Lord, did we not prophesy in your name?'" (Matt. 7:22). Injustice often appropriates the language of right causes and the hardest place to spot that gap is in those of which we are a part.

I may not conflate God's work and the national interest in the ways my spiritual and national forebears did, but my own heart still needs to confront the truth of its own complicity in injustice. "You never ask questions," Bob Dylan reminds us, "when God is on your side." And, for all of my Canadian niceness, I wasn't really asking questions.

To affirm that God entered history, that the Word "became flesh and lived among us" (John 1:14), is no sanitized claim. Histories of colonization, complex enough on their own, find greater complexity where they intersect with religious convictions. More complicated still is when they are the religious convictions that I happen to share. Yet the biblical call for justice does not stop with just calling out civil religion when it is complicit in systemic injustice; there remains a genuine hope for a true and better providence when God *will* be with us, "just as you have said."

I remain convinced that the antidote to injustice, even injustice done in the name of the Christian God, lies within the biblical tradition. Pastor, liturgist, and activist Sandra Maria Van Opstal recently proclaimed that "what has been done in the name of Christ can only be undone in the name of Christ." Or, as Amos states bluntly: "Seek good and not evil." Rather than smugly assuming "God is on our side," may we be attentive to where the God of justice already is.

REFLECTION AND DISCUSSION

1. When is it legitimate for us to say that "God is on our side" or "God is with us"?
2. Are there other examples where "just as you have said" might ring true in our lives?

FURTHER STUDY

You can read more about Canada's Truth and Reconciliation Commission at www.trc.ca and Orange Shirt Day at www.orangeshirtday .org. On Christianity and indigenous cultures, see Steven Heinrichs, ed., *Buffalo Shout, Salmon Cry: Conversations on Creation, Land Justice, and Life Together*, and Randy Woodley, *Shalom and the Community of Creation: An Indigenous Vision*.

PRAYER

God of truly right causes, align our hearts and our actions with yours. May Christ's command that our "yes be yes" and our "no be no" include our calls for you to be with us. Lord, in word, thought, and deed may we be people who seek good and not evil, people who are alive to the reality that you are a God of justice. Amen.

"Let Justice Roll Down"

Amos 5:18-24

Karen J. Johnson

> But let justice roll down like waters,
> and righteousness like an ever-flowing stream.
>
> (Amos 5:24)

G. K. Chesterton, the British author, observed in a Father Brown book, "It isn't that they can't see the solution. It is that they can't see the problem." How do we learn to see? Reading history can loosen the reins of the tyranny of the present, and of the tyranny of our own geographical, socioeconomic, and even ecclesial contexts. By encountering the strangeness of the past and of others, we can see more clearly.

I am grateful that the witnesses in that great cloud surrounding us in our race (Heb. 12:1) were different from us when they walked this earth. They experienced singleness, marriage, parenthood, race, class, and even God differently. That difference is a gift, and variety within the Body of Christ can help each member love God and love others more fully.

One member of the cloud of witnesses who has helped me see God and others in a new light is John Perkins. While we are chronologically located in the same epoch, with Perkins just a little younger than the generation who fought in World War II, our racial, class, and geographic experiences are worlds apart. Perkins is an African American who grew up poor in Mississippi. Malnutrition killed his mother and a white police officer shot his brother, a war veteran, when the brother defended himself against a beating. Perkins fled Mississippi as a young man for California, where he found economic success working in a foundry and as a union organizer. He also, unexpectedly, found Jesus.

But Jesus' call on Perkins' life was not an easy one. Jesus called Perkins to return to the place of his suffering, to the place where the violence of racial discrimination left him weeping and angry, to Mississippi. He and his wife, Vera Mae Perkins, moved back in 1960. In Mississippi, where churches that hosted civil rights activities were bombed, where civil rights leaders were killed and their murderers were not brought to justice, Perkins shared the gospel. He also worked for black empowerment, making himself a target for imprisonment and beatings. Yet by God's grace, Perkins did not harden his heart to white people. Instead, he became a leader in a movement for reconciliation and justice across racial lines.

God's grace led me to John Perkins and his autobiography, *Let Justice Roll Down*. Before learning about Perkins, I never knew someone who had been so far down on the underside of America's racial order. I had grown up in a white evangelical church in the late twentieth century, did not have to worry about money, and lived in the Midwest, which appeared to have no racial issues.

Perkins' story made me think differently, made me see my context more clearly, because his experience was so different from my own. His autobiography's title comes from one of Perkins' favorite verses, Amos 5:24. I knew very little about justice, maybe because I knew very few people who needed to experience justice. Before Perkins, I read this verse—and all the other calls for justice throughout the Scriptures—in a way that emphasized personal righteousness. Now I know that the prophetic literature does not separate righteousness from justice and righteousness. I cannot, nor can churches, seek righteousness without seeking justice, and vice versa.

The text surrounding this verse is terrifying—the Lord of Hosts tells Israel that he hates their feasts, their solemn assemblies, their playing at religion. God wants his people to let the abundant waters of justice and righteousness flow everywhere, making everything wet. Israel, to whom Amos preached, did not participate in this heavenly flood, and as a consequence the Israelites suffered a brutal exile from the land.

I am a Gentile grafted into Israel. God has not changed, though, and he wants his people, me included, to let justice roll down like waters, righteousness like an ever-flowing stream. In the United States, the church has fallen short on racial matters; it has missed the mark, which is sin. But I join John Perkins in believing that "there is no institution on earth more equipped or more capable of bringing transformation to the cause of reconciliation than the church." May we walk by the Spirit to bring justice and righteousness in our day.

REFLECTION AND DISCUSSION

1. When have you seen your context, yourself, or your past in a new light? How did that change your thoughts and actions?
2. Who is God prompting you to reach out to, to see your context more clearly? This could be someone in the past or someone who is alive now.
3. How could stepping into a different Christian context change how you encounter God? Love others?

FURTHER STUDY

In addition to *Let Justice Roll Down* (first published in 1976), I recommend John Perkins' 2018 book, *One Blood: Parting Words to the Church on Race and Love.*

PRAYER

Lord God, help us to love you enough to humble ourselves before one another, confessing those things that we have said and done that have damaged our brothers and sisters. Help us to conquer the fears that have paralyzed us for generations; help us to wash one another's wounds and become the healing community that you died for.

(From John Perkins, *One Blood: Parting Words to the Church on Race and Love.* © Moody Publishers, 2018. Used by permission.)

The New Testament

The Meek

Matthew 5:1-6

Jay R. Case

> Blessed are the meek, for they will inherit the earth.
>
> (Matt. 5:5)

The Karen (kah-rén) people were in a tight spot in the 1830s. A semi-nomadic, minority people group who lived in the remote hills of Burma, the Karen had often faced adversity at the hands of the kingdom's dominant Burman people. Now, they had another reason to worry. Burmese officials believed the British might be encouraging alliances with the Karen. Great Britain had already colonized coastal regions of Burma and looked to conquer more territory in the 1830s.

Burmese magistrates felt particularly unsettled because a remarkable movement of Christianity had emerged among the Karen. After American missionaries baptized the first Karen in 1828, Karen evangelists spearheaded a movement that produced more than a thousand baptisms and an additional four thousand professions of faith in the 1830s. Burmese government officials, perceiving these Karen as threats to their authority, arrested Christians and ordered them to renounce their faith. Magistrates placed burdensome fines on Christian villages, which sometimes provoked starvation. Karen

Christians who were found with books were beaten and jailed. Some were killed.

Elisha Abbott, an American Baptist missionary who had arrived in 1835, discovered that his very association with Karen Christians put them in danger. So he relocated from central Burma to the British-controlled coast in 1839, distressed that he had to leave behind fledgling Karen Christian congregations. Seeking to protect their well-being, Elisha Abbott urged the Karen Christians to lie low.

They refused. Over the next few years, dozens of Karen evangelists repeatedly took arduous journeys—some lasting twelve days—to reach Abbott for theological and biblical instruction. Hundreds more traveled to the missionary to be baptized.

One evangelist, Shway Bo, managed to elude Burmese magistrates who attempted to apprehend him before he made it over to British-controlled territory. But Shway Bo realized that the officials might retaliate against his Karen village. Telling Abbott he needed to hand himself over to the authorities, Shway Bo returned and was arrested. Under interrogation, a magistrate tried to get him to renounce his new faith. Shway Bo refused. The official said he should not, then, evangelize or preach. Shway Bo said nothing to this and, thankfully, was released.

Abbott asked another Karen evangelist who had been jailed and beaten whether he was angry. "No," replied the man. "I told them they might beat me to death, if they wished, but they would not make me angry, and that I should live again at the resurrection."

Even at first glance, we can see the Christian faith powerfully at work in these Karen Christians. Historical thinking, however, helps us gain an even deeper sense of the Kingdom of God at work.

We do not use the word "meek" much today, even though the word appears often in the Bible. Our avoidance of the term is not surprising. In our culture, meekness conjures up images of passivity, helplessness, and weakness. But the medieval theologian Thomas Aquinas helps us see this is a distorted definition of meekness. Aquinas understood meekness to be self-possession and fortitude when adversity strikes. Instead of lashing out or striking back in anger, the meek direct their energy and anger toward good.

Shway Bo voluntarily handed himself over to government officials to protect his village. Meekness? Yes. Passivity, helplessness, and weakness? Not by a long shot.

Indeed, the meekness of the Karen Christians helped bring about historical change. The impact here was not, as we might expect, primarily upon the Burmese authorities. Instead, it transformed the missionaries. Impressed with the dedication, perseverance, and strength of the Karen evangelists, Elisha Abbott began urging his Baptist missionary agency to grant ordination to the Karen evangelists.

This was not an obvious step. Western culture of the 1840s viewed semi-nomadic people like the Karen as "uncivilized." In fact, Abbott's proposal sparked a debate within Baptist missionary circles. Some worried that in their poorly educated and uncivilized state, Karen Christians would lead the young movement astray.

But the missionaries ultimately decided to ordain Karen evangelists. This decision not only strengthened Karen Christianity (which is still vibrant today), but also set a precedent for granting authority to local Christian leaders in other mission fields around the world.

In the mysterious workings of the Kingdom of God, the meek were inheriting the earth.

REFLECTION AND DISCUSSION

1. Where and when are we individually or collectively most likely to lash out or strike back in anger?

2. How would meekness help us to direct our energies toward what God would have us do in these situations?

FURTHER STUDY

I write at greater length about Karen Christianity in the second chapter of my book, *An Unpredictable Gospel: American Evangelicals and World Christianity, 1812–1920.* Thomas Aquinas' definition of meekness can be found in Part 2B of *The Summa Theologica,* Question 157.

PRAYER

O Lord, when we face injustice, adversity, or oppression, do not allow us to strike back in vengeance or misdirected anger. Give us grace, as you did these Karen Christians, to act with fortitude, courage, and love.

Seek the Way of Peace

Matthew 5:7-12

Jared S. Burkholder

Blessed are the peacemakers, for they will be called children of God.

(Matt. 5:9)

On November 24, 1755, ten Moravians were massacred by Native Americans during what is popularly called the French and Indian War, a conflict between England and France for control of North America. The Moravians, members of a Pietist movement that began in what is today Germany, were missionaries stationed at Gnadenhütten (now Lehighton) in Pennsylvania. The attack was just one of numerous instances of violence that took place on the disputed frontier that lay between the British colonies along the eastern seaboard and French settlements around the Great Lakes. The borderlands between the warring British and French empires were fraught with violence as frustrated settlers attacked Native Americans, who—sympathetic to the French—did the same.

The massacre was devastating to the Moravians, and it left one of their leaders, August Spangenberg, facing a moral dilemma. As settlers and Indians alike fled toward the larger Moravian settlements of Nazareth and Bethlehem for protection, many believed these towns would also be attacked. What should he do? How were Christians to promote peace in this violent world?

Spangenberg was not the first, of course, to wrestle with the moral ambiguity that instances of violence might raise. Throughout history, Christians have tried to figure out how best to live out the call to be peacemakers. We have often failed. Christians have contributed to or even served as the principal cause of conflict and discord. Some have sought to limit violence to "just causes"; others have shunned participation in the world's power structures and all forms of violence. But even Christian pacifists have come down along a spectrum of positions when considering the myriad of circumstances that might make the application of force more redeeming.

In the eighteenth century, Moravians were conscious of the Christian responsibility to promote peace. Some (though not all) refused to bear arms. Moravian leaders promoted political impartiality and valued harmony with all people—including Native Americans. They also knew that one's citizenship in the Kingdom of God was more important than colonial allegiances. But could violence be used for self-defense? For protecting the innocent? In a world filled with conflict and discord, it is easy to affirm the virtue of peacemaking, but quite another matter to find clarity in the application.

After the attack at Gnadenhütten, Spangenberg searched his soul for the right thing to do. One of his highest priorities was protecting the throngs of war-torn refugees, so he decided to have palisades constructed around Bethlehem and posted armed guards. He also gathered weapons. It is possible to view these actions as hypocritical—a point made by no less a figure than Benjamin Franklin. But Spangenberg believed it was his pastoral duty to protect the innocent refugees and hoped the display of defense would deter an attack without inciting undue violence. He directed guards to fire warning shots into the air, trying to wound the enemy only so they could be brought in and nursed back to health.

In the end, an attack never came. Perhaps Spangenberg's efforts worked as intended.

Most of us may never find ourselves in the crossfire of warring nations or caring for refugees on imperial frontiers. Still, there is much reflection to be done. Perhaps we recognize, like Spangenberg did, that the Christian commitment to peacemaking is fraught with tensions and moral dilemmas. Yet we must not let the difficulty of the task keep us from engaging necessary questions. Let us consider how we can serve as peacemakers in the midst of our own society's violence and strife.

REFLECTION AND DISCUSSION

1. How can we support policies (governmental or otherwise) that uplift the oppressed, protect the innocent, and empower the marginalized?
2. What does it look like to apply principles of nonviolence in our culture today?
3. Do we, like the Moravians, strive to place our loyalty to God's Kingdom above national interests, partisan politics, or ethno-centrism?

FURTHER STUDY

An accessible book that explores these questions further in a thoughtful and inspiring way is *Choosing Against War: A Christian View*, by the Mennonite historian John Roth. For a more academic treatment of the 1755 Gnadenhütten massacre and Spangenberg's response, consult my 2012 article in *The Journal of Moravian History*, "Neither 'Kriegerisch' nor 'Quäkerisch': Moravians and the Question of Violence in Eighteenth-Century Pennsylvania."

PRAYER

God, grant us creativity, prayerfulness, and wisdom to seek the way of peace. May you replace the desire to defeat and dominate others with a yearning in us for acts of service, radical love, and reconciliation.

This Little Light of Mine

Matthew 5:13-16

Heath W. Carter

> In the same way, let your light shine before others, so that they
> may see your good works and give glory to your Father in heaven.
>
> (Matt. 5:16)

I cannot tell you how often I sang "This Little Light of Mine" grow-ing up. We inevitably went through all the verses, complete with hand motions: *Hide it under a bushel? No! I'm gonna let it shine.* I spent the early years of my life in Kansas, and there was usually a verse about where we lived too: *Shine All Over Topeka, I'm gonna let it shine.*

As a young boy growing up in evangelical churches in the heart-land, I knew just what the lyrics meant. The light was the good news that Jesus had died for my sins. I had this light and I moreover had an individual responsibility to share it with others: *Hide it under a bushel? No!*

The song meant even more than I knew. Decades later I discov-ered that "This Little Light of Mine" was not just a Sunday School song. It was also a civil rights anthem.

"Can't sing? Sing louder!" went the refrain. "You can't just sing 'This Little Light of Mine,'" explains southern black activist Rutha Mae Harris. "You gotta shout it."

When Harris and other freedom fighters shouted the song, they were not just proclaiming their individual responsibility. They were engaging in collective witness.

The very act of singing together generated strength and courage. Looking back, Harris recalls, "Music was an anchor. It kept us from being afraid. You start singing a song, and somehow, those billy clubs would not hit you."

No one summoned collective courage like Fannie Lou Hamer did. One dark evening in 1962, just outside Indianola, Mississippi, a deputy sheriff pulled over a bus full of activists who had spent the day trying to register to vote. He arrested the driver for driving a bus that was the wrong color and was menacing the rest of the passengers when Hamer's powerful voice broke through the night: *This little light of mine, I'm going to let it shine.*

Can you imagine what the song meant in that moment?

In the context of the civil rights movement, "This Little Light of Mine" took on whole different valences than it had in my churches growing up. Black activists sang it against injustice: *Deep Down in the South, I'm going to let it shine. We've got the light of Freedom, I'm going to let it shine.* And even more specifically, they sang of the notorious sheriff of Dallas County, Alabama: *Tell Jim Clark, I'm going to let it shine. Tell the KKK, I'm going to let it shine. Tell the President, I'm going to let it shine.*

During a time when many white people presumed their innate superiority and were dead certain that there was nothing but darkness in the souls of civil rights activists, the song testified to the truth that God's love and light shone just as brightly through the lives of those Jim Crow deemed less than: *This little light of mine, I'm going to let it shine.*

There is nothing inherently contradictory between the way I sang the song growing up, with an emphasis on personal responsibility, and the way civil rights activists sang it, with an emphasis on collective witness. But to be honest, the latter meaning never really occurred to me during my early years, despite the fact that it seems to be clearly implied in Matthew 5:13-16.

In this text Jesus is not speaking to one person but to a crowd of his disciples. When he said, "You are the salt of the earth," he may well have meant "you" singular, but there is no question he meant "you" plural. He could well have said, "*Y'all* are the salt of the earth."

And moreover, y'all are the light of the world. Jesus follows up that second metaphor with a sentence that drives home the collective sense, imagining his disciples as being like "a city built on a hill [that] cannot be hid."

Both salt and light have the power to permeate and to transform, and Jesus makes it clear that his followers will be good for others so long as, collectively, they don't lose their saltiness; they will illumine the whole metaphorical house so long as, collectively, they don't hide their light under a bushel.

Today, don't forget: it's not just you that is the light of the world. It's y'all. So, let y'all's light shine!

REFLECTION AND DISCUSSION

1. What can we learn from the testimony of believers like Rutha Mae Harris and Fannie Lou Hamer?
2. How might your local church witness *collectively* to God's love and justice?

FURTHER STUDY

Eric Deggans talked to Rutha Mae Harris and other civil rights activists in an NPR episode on "This Little Light of Mine" in 2018 (www.npr.org/2018/08/06/630051651/american-anthem-this-little-light-of-mine-resistance). You can learn more about religion and the civil rights movement in Charles Marsh's *God's Long Summer: Stories of Faith and Civil Rights*.

PRAYER

God, grant us the creativity and the boldness to find ways for our lights to shine brightly together, all for the sake of your glory and our neighbor's good.

Walking in Faith Amid the Storm

Matthew 14:22-33

Rick Ostrander

> But when [Peter] noticed the strong wind, he became frightened, and beginning to sink, he cried out, "Lord, save me!" Jesus immediately reached out his hand and caught him, saying to him, "You of little faith, why did you doubt?" When they got into the boat, the wind ceased. And those in the boat worshiped him, saying, "Truly you are the Son of God."
>
> (Matt. 14:30-33)

It's a story we know well. The disciples are in a boat on the Sea of Galilee being tossed about by a storm. Jesus walks out to them on the water, and once the disciples get over their shock and realize that Jesus isn't a ghost, Peter decides to walk to him. Things go well until Peter notices his surroundings, becomes frightened (understandably so), and begins to sink until Jesus snatches him up.

I used to think the point of this story was to provide comfort during those occasional seasons when life is tumultuous; that after a few moments of Peter performing this party game trick of walking on top of the water, he would either climb back into the safety of the boat or make it to Jesus and hop up on his back, grateful for surviving the exciting adventure.

The older I get, however, the more I wonder about that interpretation. I wonder if perhaps the "wind and the waves" state, not the boat, is the natural condition of the Christian life here on earth; that our purpose isn't so much to get back in the boat or to reach Jesus' hand, but simply to learn to trust that his presence will hold us up amid the uncertainty which is a constant part of life.

That seems to be the message of a famous hymn based on this text, "Be Still, My Soul." The hymn was penned by an eighteenth-century German Pietist hymn writer by the name of Katharina von Schlegel. "Be still my soul," von Schlegel wrote, "the waves and wind still know His voice, who ruled them while He dwelt below." As you read the text of this memorable hymn, you get the idea that for von Schlegel, the resolution of the storm—the safety and security—doesn't come until the end of life. "Be still, my soul," she concludes. "When change and tears are past, all safe and blessed we shall meet at last."

When I think of Christians who have demonstrated a deep sense of trust amid constant uncertainty, another German comes to mind: Dietrich Bonhoeffer, the pastor-theologian and anti-Nazi conspirator. Bonhoeffer grew up in a prominent Prussian family and could have enjoyed a life of security as a theology professor. His Christian convictions, however, led him to become a leader in the Confessing Church movement, which opposed the capitulation of German Christianity to Nazi control.

In 1939, as conditions in Germany became increasingly dangerous for resisters, the perfect "boat" presented itself for Bonhoeffer—a faculty position at Union Theological Seminary in New York City, where he could advocate on behalf of the Confessing Church. Bonhoeffer left for the United States in June 1939, but he soon concluded that he was called to endure the ordeal of World War II back home with his fellow Germans. Two weeks later, he boarded a very different boat—the last steamer traveling to Western Europe. Bonhoeffer's opposition to the Nazis during the war years, including involvement in a failed plot to assassinate Hitler, resulted in a life of constant danger and uncertainty until his execution in April 1945. His writings, however, express a trust in God's sovereignty and ultimate victory, a faith that enabled him to walk amid the turbulent waves in his life.

A half-century later, another theologian, Henri Nouwen, followed Jesus' call out of the boat when he left a tenured position at Yale to work at a home for mentally disabled adults. About Matthew 14, Nouwen wrote:

> So much is going on in our lives: new directions, old fears, apprehensions, and great uncertainties. . . . There is so much going on beneath our feet that we are wondering if we can keep walking on all these waves. But Jesus is with us here and now. Problems are small and fears bearable when we know who calls us. . . . We will not succeed if we stay in the boat. We will not survive if we look down at the waves. But we do not have to look down and drown. Jesus calls us to look up and forward to the one who stands in the midst of the storm.

The notion of a safe, secure life is a myth. Fortunately, we have examples of Christians who have faced change and uncertainty with confidence, and we have a Savior who promises to uphold us amid the storms of life.

REFLECTION AND DISCUSSION

1. What events in your life tempt you to look away from Jesus to the wind and waves?
2. What habits can you develop to keep your gaze fixed on Jesus amid these events?

FURTHER STUDY

Among the many books that have been written about Dietrich Bonhoeffer, a good, readable introduction to his life is Michael Van Dyke's *Radical Integrity: The Story of Dietrich Bonhoeffer*. Henri Nouwen's *Discernment: Reading the Signs of Daily Life* recounts his journey from tenured professor to working with the disabled, and is a wise reflection on what it means to follow Christ amid life's changes.

PRAYER

Heavenly Father, we know that you hold all things in your sovereign hand and that you work for our ultimate good. Help us to trust in your love and your faithfulness and to fix our eyes on Jesus, the author and finisher of our faith, who upholds us amid the uncertainties of life. Amen.

Grit and Faith

Matthew 15:21-28

Beth Allison Barr

> [The Canaanite woman] came and knelt before [Jesus], saying, "Lord, help me." He answered, "It is not fair to take the children's food and throw it to the dogs." She said, "Yes, Lord, yet even the dogs eat the crumbs that fall from their masters' table." Then Jesus answered her, "Woman, great is your faith! Let it be done for you as you wish." And her daughter was healed instantly.
>
> (Matt. 15:25-28)

Grit is a hot topic on college campuses. In a *Psychology Today* blog post, for example, Peter Gray warned that many college students not only view lower grades as failure but "interpret such 'failure' as the end of the world." Instead of persisting, they give up—which seems to correlate with current college retention statistics: one out of every three college freshman in the United States drop out. So psychologist Angela Duckworth has argued that "grit"—perseverance and passion for long term goals—is a better predictor of success than IQ or family income. Students who learn to persist despite challenges and even failures experience greater success.

I find modern conversations about grit especially fascinating because they remind me of the Woman of Canaan in late medieval English sermons. By the fifteenth century, the Woman of Canaan had become a story frequently included in sermons preached to ordinary people. Matthew 15:21-28 was the Gospel reading for the Second Sunday of Lent in the most popular medieval liturgical cycle in England, so it is understandable how often the story appeared in Lenten sermons. Instead of focusing on her as a foreigner, or on how Jesus calls her a bad name (dog), or even her role as a mother, late medieval English sermons focus on her persistence—her grit.

Just think about the sequence of events. The woman finds Jesus and starts trying to get his attention. But Jesus ignores her. The disciples try to send her away. When Jesus finally does answer her, he tells her no. When she begs him for help, he insults her. But instead of giving up and going away, she stands her ground. She answers Jesus back, challenging him to help her. It is only at this point, after her refusal to give up, that Jesus finally relents. "Woman," he says, "great is your faith! Let it be done for you as you wish."

I love how one English friar described the Woman of Canaan: "She prayed with great perseverance for she rested not till Christ granted her what she asked. Also she prayed with great humility and great peace for she asked not for riches nor praise nor vengeance for her enemies nor help for herself but only mercy that her daughter might be delivered of the demon." The sermon text then states—and this is the really striking part—that unlike St. Paul, who cried to God for his "thorn of the flesh" to be removed but God "would not hear his prayer" (2 Cor. 12:7-9), God "granted this woman her asking."

The Woman of Canaan persevered in her faith. She believed that Jesus could heal her daughter, and she refused to give up despite the challenges she faced. And Jesus praised her! "Woman, great is your faith!"

When medieval Christians in England heard this story, they heard Jesus praise a woman for her determination. They heard Jesus reward a woman for persisting despite obstacles and even initial failure. They heard Jesus answer the prayers of the woman and heal her daughter. They heard a story focused on how a woman refused to give up and how her actions were praised by God.

We call this grit. Medieval Christians called it faith.

REFLECTION AND DISCUSSION

1. How do you respond to failure? What helps you to persevere?
2. Is persistence a virtue for Christians? What other biblical stories reinforce the value of persistence?

FURTHER STUDY

You can find Peter Gray's 2015 post on "Declining Student Resilience" at www.psychology today.com/blog. Look for Angela Lee Duckworth's talk on "Grit: The Power of Passion and Perseverance" at www.ted.com/talks. You can also find further discussion about medieval female spirituality in Beth Allison Barr's "'The Faith of women . . . was the beginning of salvation': Faith and Women in Late Medieval English Sermons," coming Fall 2020 in *Fides et Historia*.

PRAYER

God be in my head and in my understanding
   In mine Eyes; and in my looking
   In my Mouth; and in my speaking
   In my Heart; and in my thinking
   At my end, and in my departing. Amen.

   (From a sixteenth-century prayer book)

Learning in Wartime

Matthew 24:1-14

Margaret Bendroth

Jesus answered them, "Beware that no one leads you astray. For many will come in my name, saying, 'I am the Messiah!' and they will lead many astray. And you will hear of wars and rumors of wars; see that you are not alarmed; for this must take place, but the end is not yet. . . . And because of the increase of lawlessness, the love of many will grow cold. But the one who endures to the end will be saved. And this good news of the kingdom will be proclaimed throughout the world, as a testimony to all the nations; and then the end will come."

(Matt. 24:4-6, 12-14)

Who doesn't appreciate a sense of urgency, especially in other people? What's not to love about a fellow human being who knows not to hog the sidewalk, staring into a cellphone as if awaiting a word from God, who resists chatting up the cashier when others are standing in line?

It's a dangerous habit for a historian, however. Archival research can take hours of shuffling through meaningless paper before any of it makes sense, before a story finally manifests itself. Good ideas need lots of time: hours of idle contemplation, long walks, and long conversations. They can't be rushed or hurried.

All that intellectual foot dragging goes against the spirit of the times, though. Any decent person who reads the news has to wonder if our days may well be numbered. Our leaders seem to relish careening toward one disaster after another, without an end in view. We hear of wars and rumors of wars—and of melting icebergs and rising seas. We hear of persecution and hate and betrayal and, yes, the love of many does seem to have grown cold.

We can understand now, perhaps better than any previous generation, the bottomless anxiety that C. S. Lewis addressed in 1939, in a sermon given at Oxford, entitled "Learning in Wartime." He was speaking to young men expecting to go into battle, fathers who would watch them leave, possibly for good, and older men who knew all too well the horrors in store. With the Great War barely over, Britain was gearing up yet again for privation and sacrifice, for rationing and long lines and unspeakable loss.

At a time like this, what could be more self-indulgent—and foolish—than reading ancient books, or burying oneself in an archive? Or, as Lewis put the question, "What is the use of beginning a task which we have so little chance of finishing? Or, even if we ourselves should happen not to be interrupted by death or military service, why should we—indeed *how* can we—continue to take an interest in these placid operations when the lives of our friends and the liberties of Europe are in the balance?"

Lewis found spiritual comfort in the historical long view. "Human life has always been lived on the edge of a precipice," he said. If our ancestors had postponed the search for "knowledge and beauty" until all was secure, "the search would never have begun."

"Most of all," said Lewis, "we need intimate knowledge of the past. Not that the past has any magic about it, but because we cannot study the future, and yet need something to set against the present," to remind us that what seems utterly certain today is "merely temporary fashion."

Lewis was not arguing for an effete, high-minded retreat from the present, as if scholarship—even the very best—was some holy end in itself. But he was clear that the times required more than just a casual acquaintance with the past, as if it were a hobby or a distraction, beloved by history "buffs" but ignored by everyone else. People on the brink of world war needed a deep and thoughtful engagement with their ancestors, an "intimate knowledge" of those who had gone before. They needed to know that the future would be neither completely terrible nor wonderfully perfect. It would be just as morally complex and frustratingly inconclusive as the past and present had been.

History cannot provide certainty. Though it may give us moments of inspiration, shining examples of people who made it through hard times, it throws out many more stories of people who failed miserably or fell victim to horror and despair. History's gift is what it allows us to see: our place within the vast column of time. It is the truest way of knowing, as Lewis' contemporary Evelyn Underhill wrote, that "our personal ups and downs," and even the screaming newspaper headlines of the day, are "small and transitory spiritual facts, within a vast abiding spiritual world." An "intimate knowledge of the past" opens to us not just the incalculable wealth of human experience; it is the closest we can come to a "God's-eye view" of our world, as it is now and as it may become.

REFLECTION AND DISCUSSION

1. How are our times similar to Lewis' and Underhill's? How are they different?
2. Are there limits on "learning in wartime"? Are there certain subjects or lines of investigation that historians should avoid or are obligated to pursue?

FURTHER STUDY

Lewis' "Learning in Wartime" sermon was republished as part of *The Weight of Glory*. Read more from Evelyn Underhill in *The Spiritual Life*.

PRAYER

O God, thank you that prayer turns us from the chaotic, bewildering surface of life to its unchanging deeps, and a faithful adherence to you. But even as our prayers bring us into your abiding presence and peace, we have the sacred privilege to carry the torment and sorrow of the world with us, and to submit it by prayer to your redeeming action. Keep our love from growing cold and strengthen us to proclaim the good news of your kingdom throughout the world. Amen.

(Based on Evelyn Underhill, "The Spiritual Life in War-time")

"Who Can Be Saved?"

Mark 10:17-31

Jemar Tisby

> Then Jesus looked around and said to his disciples, "How hard it
> will be for those who have wealth to enter the kingdom of God!"
> And the disciples were perplexed at these words. But Jesus said
> to them again, "Children, how hard it is to enter the kingdom
> of God! It is easier for a camel to go through the eye of a needle
> than for someone who is rich to enter the kingdom of God."
> They were greatly astounded and said to one another, "Then who
> can be saved?" Jesus looked at them and said, "For mortals it is
> impossible, but not for God; for God all things are possible."
>
> (Mark 10:23-27)

Our lack of progress on the journey of racial justice is often, simply and sadly, a function of money. Not to say that it's only about
money, but so often the pace of change around the topic of race is
slowed down because of the financial risks associated with publicly
confronting it.

In 1667 the Virginia Assembly, a group of white Anglican men,
passed a law saying that "the conferring of baptisme [sic] doth not
alter the condition of the person as to his bondage or ffreedome
[sic]." In other words, baptizing an enslaved African, Native American, or person of mixed-race heritage would not emancipate them.

Why was such a law remarkable? First, it had been the custom in England that Christians should not enslave other Christians. The law passed by the Virginia Assembly codified a practice that was, at best, questionable in their home country.

Second, the preamble to the law states the immediate reason for its supposed necessity. Plantation owners had raised the concern about manumission. If baptism required freeing their enslaved "property," then how would they make money? The men of the Virginia Assembly passed the law so "that diverse masters, ffreed [sic] from this doubt, may more carefully endeavor the propagation of Christianity." In a backwards way, by making it harder for people to gain their freedom, these white Christians intended to ease the way for evangelism. The primary concern, however, was assuaging the fears of people who trafficked in human bondage to increase their bottom line.

Jesus confronts the contradiction between gripping a fistful of dollars and holding tight to the gospel. In Mark 10, a young man asks Jesus, "What must I do to inherit eternal life?" (v. 17).

Jesus rattles off a list of answers that any pre-bar mitzvah Jewish child could easily recite. Then Jesus gets to the heart of the matter. "You lack one thing," he said. "Go, sell what you own, and give the money to the poor, and you will have treasure in heaven; then come, follow me" (v. 21).

It is not until the man walks away sad that we learn he is a man of great wealth.

What upsets this man so much? Surely the prospect of selling his material possessions and giving away the proceeds to the needy had the man picturing scenes of his own prospective neediness and simple lifestyle. Not only material comforts were at stake, though. The prestige of being known as a rich person was also on the line. What would people think of him if he had no remarkable wealth? Would he be able to stay in the same social circles, get seated in the places of honor, have a voice in the community's political deliberations?

For all of this, the man went away sad.

Then Jesus turns to the disciples—he turns to us—and makes explicit the lesson with which he challenged the man: "How hard it will be for those who have wealth to enter the kingdom of God! . . . It is easier for a camel to go through the eye of a needle than for someone who is rich to enter the kingdom of God" (vv. 23-24).

We know our own temptations when it comes to wealth. Money entangles. It winds around our hearts and chokes out generosity, compassion, and even love for God. After all, you cannot serve both God and Mammon (Matt. 6:24).

This is what has happened in the church with regard to racial justice. As we study history, we find that time and again Christians valued the material currency of money more than the spiritual currency of the gospel.

Think of the institutions with which you are affiliated. Do they display a lack of racial and ethnic diversity? Have they failed to confront racism with the organization or in the local community? Has progress on racial justice stalled or been nonexistent?

If you dwell on these questions, it is likely you will find that some financial consideration and, more pointedly, the fear of losing money, plays an outsized role in determining the pace of racial transformation.

Can we extricate our racial reality from the influence of money, so that we can love God and neighbor more purely? Jesus says, "For mortals it is impossible, but not for God; for God all things are possible" (v. 27). So Jesus has the final word about freeing us from the love of money to more effectively fight racism, and that word is "grace."

Out of love Jesus confronts us with our idolatry of money and our fear of confronting racism. He beckons us not to try to walk this journey of racial justice in our own strength. It is impossible. But in humble dependence on the grace of God, the impossible becomes possible. By faith racial justice moves from a dream restrained by the chains of money to a reality emancipated by the love of Jesus.

REFLECTION AND DISCUSSION

1. What institution or organization are you part of right now that may be missing opportunities to pursue racial justice because of financial concerns?

2. Are you willing to give sacrificially for the cause of racial justice? To what individuals or organizations could you contribute?

FURTHER STUDY

For more on the economic history of slavery in the United States, see *Soul by Soul: Life Inside the Antebellum Slave Market* by Walter Johnson. On the continuation of "slavery by another name" after the Civil War, see Douglas Blackmon's book by that name—or the PBS documentary it inspired (pbs.org/slavery-by-another-name).

PRAYER

God Our Lord, I confess that I have remained silent in the face of racism or supported it because I valued money more than my neighbor. I have been part of organizations and institutions that have traded human dignity for a dollar.

I repent of my fear of loss, and ask you to replace it with faith in Christ. Help me, by the power of the Holy Spirit, to courageously confront racism in all its forms, though it may cost me material benefits and monetary rewards. Give me the courage to confront those around me who would perpetuate prejudice in order to protect their own profit. Give me the compassion to side with the marginalized in standing against racial injustice.

Remind me, in your grace, that with me it is impossible, but with you, God, all things are possible. In Jesus' name, I pray. Amen.

Sky Tinged Red

Luke 1:68-79

Christopher Gehrz

By the tender mercy of our God, the dawn from on high will
break upon us, to give light to those who sit in darkness and in
the shadow of death, to guide our feet into the way of peace.

(Luke 1:78-79)

The Bible can seem to glow, it has so much imagery of light. "In your
light we see light" (Ps. 36:9) says the psalmist of a God in whose Son
"there is no darkness at all" (1 John 1:5). For Jesus is "the light of all
people," a beacon that "shines in the darkness, and the darkness did
not overcome it" (John 1:4-5). In turn, his followers are called to be
"the light of the world" (Matt. 5:14).

So I don't think one of my sunnier Christian students was ready
for the dark response he received from Dora Eiger Zaidenweber, a
Jewish survivor of both Auschwitz-Birkenau and Bergen-Belsen.
She was about ninety years old when she came to our campus to
share her story. Saddened and inspired, my student asked Dora if
the break of dawn filled her with hope. "Did the morning's light
remind you of God's unfailing goodness?" he innocently wondered.

"No," she said, curtly. On the contrary, Dora had dreaded each new day: the pale rays of dawn revealed the bodies of those who hadn't lived through the night.

That's not how Christians want to greet the light of a new day. "The dawn from on high will break upon us," proclaims Zechariah at the birth of his son, "to give light to those who sit in darkness and in the shadow of death, to guide our feet into the way of peace." Christians traditionally sing his canticle in the season of Advent, when we await Jesus' coming and know that we need not fear anything, even death.

But "we do the Light a disservice," warns social psychologist Christena Cleveland, "when we underestimate the darkness." Writing in the wake of the controversial November 2014 grand jury decision in Ferguson, Missouri, Cleveland reminded readers of her blog that

> Jesus entered a world plagued not only by the darkness of individual pain and sin, but also by the darkness of systemic oppression. Jesus' people, the Hebrews, were a subjugated people living as exiles in their own land; among other things, they were silenced, targets of police brutality, and exploitatively taxed. They were a people so beaten down by society that only a remnant . . . continued to believe that the Messianic prophecies would one day come to pass. For many, the darkness of long-standing oppression had extinguished any hope for liberation.

As people called "out of darkness into his marvelous light" (1 Pet. 2:9), we may prefer to skip ahead to the winter holiday illuminated by an angel host and a shining star. But "Advent begins in the dark," the Episcopalian preacher and writer Fleming Rutledge observes, and the "authentically *hopeful* Christmas spirit has not looked away from darkness, but straight into it."

So when those of us who follow Jesus study history, we shouldn't look too quickly for the light. When we turn to the past, we must seek truth among lengthening shadows.

In fact, the title of the book that brought Dora Eiger Zaidenweber to our campus did not evoke the rising of the sun, but its setting. *Sky Tinged Red* resulted from Dora's painstaking transliteration and translation of a Yiddish memoir that her father, Isaia Eiger, had secretly kept throughout his time in Birkenau. "Don't you see the fire and smoke," he asked the bystanders who allowed the Shoah to consume six million Jews. "The clouds and sky, tinged red?"

Dora's father bore the name of a prophet whose words give voice to suffering millions through histories ancient and recent: "justice is far from us, and righteousness does not reach us; we wait for light, and lo! there is darkness; and for brightness, but we walk in gloom" (Isa. 59:9). That God's Shalom still remains distant—that so many still sit in the shadow of death—is the fault of people much like us. Not just the terrible deeds done by the butchers of Auschwitz and other perpetrators we so easily judge, sin consists of the good left selfishly, callously undone by people like us.

When we look honestly into the dark mirror of history, most of us will find that we resemble the Christian bystanders who left Isaia Eiger screaming for someone, anyone to extinguish the holocaust consuming his people. But if we look too quickly for light in the past, we may fail to realize just what it means that "the darkness did not overcome" God's Word, Jesus Christ.

REFLECTION AND DISCUSSION

1. Which historical "darkness" do you find most convicting?
2. Which histories tempt you to look too quickly for light? What's a topic whose past you could study more patiently and diligently?

FURTHER STUDY

Learn more about Isaia Eiger's remarkable memoir—and equally remarkable daughter—at www.skytingedred.com. In addition to such published memoirs, you can also find firsthand accounts of survivors at the websites of the U.S. Holocaust Memorial Museum (www.ushmm.org) and the Shoah Foundation's Visual History Archive (https://sfi.usc.edu).

PRAYER

Merciful God, shine brightly on memories dimmed by forgetting; show us pasts we'd rather ignore. Help us to carry the light of Christ to those who sit in the darkness of our time, to ease the pain of individuals, and to end the subjugation of peoples. For Jesus' name's sake we pray. Amen.

Pondering the Past

Luke 2:1-20

Wendy Wong Schirmer

> But Mary treasured up all these things and pondered them in her heart.
>
> (Luke 2:19, NIV)

Christmas means receiving the gift of Christ himself, God Incarnate. St. Luke notes that Jesus' mother Mary thus welcomed God, and that she "pondered" and "reflected" on things, people, and events in her heart (Luke 1:29, 2:19, 2:51). For Pope Benedict XVI, she is "the silent Virgin who listens constantly to the eternal Word, who lives in the Word of God. Mary treasures in her heart the words that come from God and, piecing them together as in a mosaic, learns to understand them."

In so receiving the gift of Christ, Mary demonstrates that receptivity need not be passive, sentimental, or credulous. She actively contemplates, sifts, and discerns what she takes in, making her the model intellectual. She employs her intellect as historian Richard Hofstadter defines it: "the critical, creative, and contemplative side of the mind. Whereas intelligence seeks to grasp, manipulate, re-order, adjust, intellect examines, *ponders*, wonders, theorizes, criticizes, [and] imagines."

In so receiving the gift of Christ, the intellectual Mary is also willing to encounter. In a meditation "for a culture of encounter," Pope Francis describes a Christ-like encounter as "not just seeing, but looking; not just hearing, but listening; not just passing people by, but stopping with them; not just saying 'what a shame, poor people!' but allowing yourself to be moved with compassion."

Encounter in the study of history means learning to navigate a foreign country. While researching the building of Philadelphia's Cathedral of Saints Peter and Paul, I came across St. John Neumann, one of three bishops of Philadelphia who oversaw the building of a cathedral that would unify and cement a Catholic presence there. Not only did I have to familiarize myself with a different period and historiography, but Neumann himself taught me something about receptivity and encounter: a native of Bohemia, he was an immigrant ministering to Catholic immigrants—a stranger tasked with welcoming the stranger amid the Nativist Riots of the 1830s and 1840s. Unsurprisingly, Neumann felt discouragement. He asked to be replaced as bishop, but Pope Pius IX asked him to continue, so Neumann pressed on.

As a non-American who studies early U.S. history and often teaches difficult topics like slavery and its aftermath to non-humanities majors, I know discouragement too. My students and I read John Steinbeck's visceral depiction of the 1960 New Orleans desegregation crisis in *Travels With Charley*, and we learn the tragedy of history. But our subsequent reading of Martin Luther King Jr.'s "I Have a Dream" speech convicts me for staring into the darkness but forgetting to see grace and hope—namely, what's possible when trusting God and not relying on my own strength. I learn again to press on, receiving God's gift in my encounter with the foreignness of the past.

By receiving the Word of God like Mary, we learn to see all things in the light of Christ, the past included. We learn not to mistake hope for optimism or merely to curse the darkness: Jesus descended into Hell and then rose from the dead. Treasuring up our encounters—including difficult ones—and pondering them in our hearts lets us appreciate the work of navigating and making sense of the past that we find challenging and necessary.

REFLECTION AND DISCUSSION

1. Where have you let fear or undue optimism, haste, or a desire for comfort get in the way of understanding? How might you ponder something in the past?
2. How has an encounter with history felt most like learning to navigate a foreign country?

FURTHER STUDY

Pope Benedict XVI reflects on St. Luke's account of Jesus' birth in *Mary and Jesus of Nazareth: The Infancy Narratives*. To learn more about the life of St. John Neumann, visit the National Shrine of St. John Neumann (stjohnneumann.org) and the Redemptorist archives (redemptorists.net/redemptorists/archives). For a good primer on the study of history as a way of knowing, see John Tosh, *The Pursuit of History*.

PRAYER

Breathe in me, O Holy Spirit, that my thoughts may all be holy. Act in me, O Holy Spirit, that my work, too, may be holy. Draw my heart, O Holy Spirit, that I love but what is holy. Strengthen me, O Holy Spirit, to defend all that is holy. Guard me, then, O Holy Spirit, that I always may be holy. Amen.

(St. Augustine)

Selfishness One Degree Removed

Luke 14:25-32

Kristin Kobes Du Mez

> Whoever comes to me and does not hate father and mother, wife
> and children, brothers and sisters, yes, and even life itself, cannot
> be my disciple.
>
> (Luke 14:26)

Could Jesus have meant "this drastic teaching to apply to women?"
This was the question that M. Madeline Southard pondered in her
1927 book, *The Attitude of Jesus toward Woman*. It was a question
she had struggled with her entire adult life.

Southard had grown up in the late nineteenth century, during
the height of Victorian ideals of Christian womanhood. To be a
Christian woman was first and foremost to be a wife and a mother,
to find one's identity and purpose in domestic relationships. But
Southard had never really fit this mold of respectable Christian
womanhood. Growing up on the Kansas plains, she had been influenced by holiness Methodism, and by the region's populism. Her
faith filled her with boldness and the desire to do great things for
the cause of justice and righteousness. For a short time, that meant
swinging an ax in saloons with Carrie Nation—or at least watching

as Nation swung the ax. Temperance was a cause close to Southard's heart because she saw it as a way of pursuing holiness and protecting women from male vice.

Driven by her pursuit of holiness, Southard became a preacher. She founded the International Association of Women Ministers in 1919, and she worked for the cause of women's rights within Methodist churches and within American society more broadly. Yet, throughout her life, she struggled with the question of Christian womanhood. Even as she felt called to public ministry, she longed to experience "this gift, this glory of motherhood." She poured out these longings in her personal journals; during periods of despair she sought to hold onto her faith in God's plan for her "as dying people fight for breath." Southard remained single her entire life, and she never experienced "the glories of womanhood" she had so desperately hoped would be hers. It was in attempting to reconcile her own desires and sense of calling that Southard turned to the Scriptures.

Although the Christianity of her youth had emphasized motherhood as a woman's chief end, Southard discovered that the Bible seemed to teach the very opposite. Jesus had declared that he had come to set family members against each other—not just in Luke 14, but in Matthew 10: "Whoever loves father or mother more than me is not worthy of me; and whoever loves son or daughter more than me is not worthy of me" (v. 37). In fact, Southard contended that in every single instance in the New Testament where Jesus reproved a woman, it was for her failure to subordinate her feminine interests to her interests as a citizen of God's kingdom. With his own mother (Matt. 12:48-50), with a woman in a crowd (Luke 11:27-28), with his rebuke of "the mother of the sons of Zebedee" (Matt. 20:20-28), Jesus insisted that nothing, not even a woman's devotion to her own children, should come before her devotion to Christ.

Southard believed that motherhood was a beautiful gift, and she remained convinced that there was a "marvelous and beautiful unselfishness of motherhood." Yet she warned that "every great virtue is shadowed by its special vice." By placing one's love for one's own children above one's love for Christ, and above love for all children, women had caused great harm. Indeed, a mother's ambition for her own children was really nothing more than "selfishness one degree removed." In the case of "unconsecrated motherhood," the beauty of motherhood had been perverted.

The family didn't exist for its own sake, Southard concluded. It existed to prepare people to serve God and others. If parental love didn't flow out to all children everywhere, "this pure spring of living water may fall back into its own pool to become stagnant and fetid." Domestic affections must be subordinated to devotion to Christ and enlarged to include the entire "household of faith" and humanity itself.

From a deep well of personal anguish, and through a life devoted to searching the Scriptures, Southard had found in the words and witness of Christ a pattern that contradicted the longstanding ideal of "Christian womanhood." She hoped to offer a different way forward for women of her own generation, and for women of future generations who sought to follow Christ above all.

REFLECTION AND DISCUSSION

1. Southard's life and ministry demonstrate how much our encounter with the Scriptures is shaped by our personal experiences and by the culture in which we live. How do your own experiences, and your own historical context, frame the way you approach these biblical texts?

2. Do women today still encounter cultural and religious ideals of "Christian womanhood" that run counter to the New Testament vision Christ offers women?

FURTHER STUDY

Read more about Madeline Southard's theology in her book *The Attitude of Jesus Toward Woman* (digitized at hathitrust.org), or peruse resources related to Southard and other women like her at Christians for Biblical Equality (cbeinternational.org).

PRAYER

In loving those closest to us, O God, teach us to love all our neighbors—all your children. And in loving to study the past, may we learn better to love you—with our mind, as with our heart, soul, and strength.

The Temptation of Power

Luke 22:24-38

Daniel K. Williams

> A dispute also arose among them as to which one of them was to be regarded as the greatest. But he said to them, "The kings of the Gentiles lord it over them; and those in authority over them are called benefactors. But not so with you; rather the greatest among you must become like the youngest, and the leader like one who serves. For who is greater, the one who is at the table or the one who serves? Is it not the one at the table? But I am among you as one who serves."
>
> (Luke 22:24-27)

Jesus' followers are plagued with a sinful lust for power. This was true in the first century, and it is equally true in the twenty-first.

One of the clearest indications of this universal problem is that only moments after Jesus presented his disciples with a radical teaching about servanthood and the way of the cross, the disciples immediately focused not on how they could be servants but on how many swords they might have on hand for self-defense.

If we're tempted to roll our eyes at the disciples' obtuseness, consider how many times we ourselves might have wished that our group of Christians had more political influence, or that we might get a job promotion or even a simple acknowledgement of respect for our achievements. If we are honest, we too might be a lot more comfortable wielding a metaphorical sword on our own behalf than in giving up the opportunity for earthly recognition in order to serve others in God's kingdom.

Much of my historical research focuses on American Christians' attempts to acquire and exercise political power—an all-too-frequent quest in American history, from the New England Puritans to the modern Christian Right. Christians who have acquired political influence have almost never been satisfied with the results. The social evils they thought they could stop through politics have often continued unabated, while the gospel truths they wanted to uphold have been tarnished.

The evil effects of power even on Christians should not surprise anyone who has an understanding of the corrupting influence of power on sinful human hearts. God created us to exercise delegated authority over creation as image bearers of God, but in our sin we have rebelled against the divine king by seeking to rule creation, not as stewards but as entitled owners. Our desire for power is really an attempt to make ourselves, rather than God, the ultimate king. It was because of his understanding of original sin that Lord Acton, a devout Catholic, famously said that "power tends to corrupt, and absolute power corrupts absolutely."

At some level, even secular people recognize this, which is why a lot of secular academics express great admiration for marginalized people and historically oppressed groups. But the solution they commonly propose—to take power from the oppressors and give it to the oppressed—is not likely to solve the problem of oppression for very long, because when any group achieves power, it quickly begins to abuse it. The only way for us to avoid this sin is to consciously make God's glory our sole motivation in every act of power that we exercise and to always see ourselves as servants rather than "benefactors" in our every action.

But because we never do this perfectly, our exercises of power are tainted by the sin of self-aggrandizement. This is why human power often looks so ugly.

In my study of history, I find that the people I most admire for their willingness to renounce power or suffer unjustly in one area of their lives seem much less admirable in the areas where they did exercise (and abuse) their privileged power status. George Washington's decision to give up the power of his executive office for the sake of the republic is, in my view, one of the greatest acts any American president ever took. But the areas of Washington's life where he exercised power without such restraint, such as his pursuit of runaway slaves, are far less inspiring. Similarly, Martin Luther King Jr. appears most worthy of admiration in the areas of his life where he renounced power and suffered unjustly, as he did when he chose to forego the path of a privileged academic or pastoral life and instead go to prison and ultimately give his life for the sake of justice for others. Yet in the areas of King's life where he did exercise power and abuse it—such as his displays of male chauvinism or his treatment of younger civil rights activists who mocked him as "De Lawd" for his love of recognition—he looks far less exemplary. Similarly, it is easy to sympathize with the northeastern Irish immigrants of the mid-nineteenth century when we focus on their powerless state as victims of English oppression, famine, and Anglo-American discrimination. But when we examine their violent abuse and murder of African Americans—the one group over which they exercised some power in mid-nineteenth-century America—we see that they were no more responsible with power than any other group in history.

It is easy for us to deceive ourselves into thinking that we will not abuse power, but Jesus' warning, as well as the repeated examples of power abuse that we see in history, should dissuade us of this illusion. If we are honest, we can probably think of ways in which we have abused the limited power that we already possess, whether it is the power we hold as parents, teachers, or volunteer leaders in our churches and communities.

For us, the only power that is truly safe for us to use is the power of the cross, which calls us to die to ourselves and serve others by seeking God's glory and not our own. As followers of a Savior who gave up the trappings of heavenly power in order to become a servant, we have been empowered by God to live radical lives of service rather than power-seeking.

REFLECTION AND DISCUSSION

1. What power do you possess? How are you tempted to abuse it?
2. Given the corrupting influence of power, how do you think Christians can best engage political and social problems?

FURTHER STUDY

On Jesus' power-relinquishing path to the cross, see Timothy Keller, *Jesus the King: Understanding the Life and Death of the Son of God.* For a thoughtful critique of evangelicals' quest for political power, see John Fea, *Believe Me: The Evangelical Road to Donald Trump.* And on white evangelicals' history of preserving social power for their own race at the expense of black Christians, see Jemar Tisby, *The Color of Compromise: The Truth about the American Church's Complicity in Racism.*

PRAYER

Lord, you have shown us a path to glory that the world has never recognized: the path of the cross. Help me to seek that path and not the path of recognition for my achievements. Give me the strength to resist the temptation to seek power in whatever area of my life I am seeking it, and help me to find my joy and delight in your sacrifice for me on the cross. In the spheres of authority that you have given me, help me today to be a Christ-following servant to others and not a self-seeking recognition-seeker. Forgive me for the sins that I have committed in this area, and renew me by the power of your Holy Spirit. Amen.

Hearts Strangely Warmed

John 1:1-18

David R. Swartz

> And the Word became flesh and lived among us, and we have seen his glory, the glory as of a father's only son, full of grace and truth.
>
> (John 1:14)

On May 21, 1738, Charles Wesley, recently returned from a failed missionary expedition to America, experienced Pentecost. Near St. Martin's Le Grand in London, the Spirit of God came upon him, he said, and "chased away the darkness of my unbelief." Three nights later, his brother John went very unwillingly to a religious meeting at nearby Aldersgate Street, but became transfixed. "About a quarter before nine," he confided to his diary, "while [the preacher] was describing the change which God works in the heart through faith in Christ, I felt my heart strangely warmed. I felt I did trust in Christ, Christ alone, for salvation; and an assurance was given me that He had taken away my sins, even mine, and saved me from the law of sin and death." Charles reported, "Towards ten, my brother was brought in triumph by a troop of our friends, and declared, 'I believe.' We sang the hymn with great joy, and parted with prayer."

Driven by doctrine, knowledge, and a love for logical argument in the age of Enlightenment, the scholarly brothers Wesley came to embrace spiritual realities that extended beyond reason. They began to practice "heart religion." As historian A. Skevington Wood describes it, "The cardinal tenet of the Protestant Reformation . . . now not only seized [John Wesley's] mind but touched his heart . . . It was indeed a strange warmth . . . for he was not a man given to emotional impressions." Incorporating the new spiritual experience into their Christian faith, the Wesleys would innovate a new sensibility, a new methodology, and a new movement. Formulating what came to be called the "Wesleyan quadrilateral," they added experience to reason.

Like the Wesleys, I often feel most comfortable when inhabiting my mind. I spend my days thinking and arguing and persuading more than stretching and pounding and planting. Every so often, however, I am grounded by physical realities. And even as I try to think my way to spiritual maturity, I am reminded that the very foundation of Christian faith takes embodied shape. Indeed, the Gospel narrative depicts God becoming flesh.

Living a fully human life, Jesus of Nazareth was born to a laboring mother in the throes of birthing pains. He experienced the fears of childhood, the angst of late childhood, and the temptations of mature adulthood—all (and this is where the similarities finally end) without succumbing to sin. Jesus was *Emmanuel*, God with us. "The Word became flesh," wrote the apostle for whom John Wesley was named, "and lived among us, and we have seen his glory, the glory as of a father's only son, full of grace and truth." In his "explanatory notes" on John 1:14, John Wesley describes how "flesh" often signifies "corrupt nature." He writes, "We are all by nature liars and children of wrath." And yet "by a most amazing condescension," Christ's flesh revealed glory and grace and truth in all his "tempers, ministrations, and conduct." At the "heart of the gospel of salvation is God's incarnation," says Methodist theologian William Willimon. The ineffable Yahweh was embodied in Jesus of ancient Nazareth.

The Wesleys and their followers sought to emulate Christ in life. In his attempt to practice incarnational living, the "dapper little don" (as historian A. Skevington Wood described John Wesley, who "was so very particular that he could not bear the slightest speck of dirt on his clerical attire") began preaching on the filthy coal-blackened streets of an industrializing England. He reincarnated from Oxford don to field preacher. Covering over a quarter-million miles to deliver forty thousand sermons in his lifetime, John Wesley went to the people. He generally preached in the open air: in the middle of streets, main city squares, meat markets, prisons, asylums, private homes, hostels, even on a flight of steps outside a malt house. He embraced the heckles and odors of what one contemporary called the "uncouth mob." He did so believing that rehearsing the incarnation on earth, paradoxically, could help Christians reach unearthly realms.

The Wesleys remind those of us who work at desks or in class-rooms that the stuff of the earth—hearts, bodies, space, and air—matters. Indeed, Charles' hymn "And Can It Be That I Should Gain," written immediately after his conversion in May 1738, echoed the Apostle John's invocation of "flesh" and "dwelling":

> He left His Father's throne above,
> So free, so infinite His grace!
> Emptied Himself of all but love,
> And bled for Adam's helpless race.

The language of "emptied" and "bled" is as palpable as it is conceptual. What we believe matters, but *how* we believe is just as important.

REFLECTION AND DISCUSSION

1. How do you feel what you believe?
2. In what ways might you embody Christ's love today?

FURTHER STUDY

Learn more about the Wesleys from A. Skevington Wood, *The Burning Heart: John Wesley, Evangelist* and Geordan Hammond, *John Wesley in America: Restoring Primitive Christianity*. On historical sites related to the Wesleys in Savannah and St. Simons Island in Georgia, see the website of the United Methodist Church Archives (www.gcah.org/research/travelers-guide/john-wesleys-american -parish).

PRAYER

God, our imprisoned spirits are bound in sin. But your eye diffuses a ray that fills the dungeon with light. You loose our chains and set free our hearts. Help us to rise and follow you. Amen.

A Higher Law

Acts 4

Timothy L. Wood

> Then they called them in again and commanded them not to
> speak or teach at all in the name of Jesus. But Peter and John
> replied, "Which is right in God's eyes: to listen to you, or to him?
> You be the judges! As for us, we cannot help speaking about what
> we have seen and heard."
>
> (Acts 4:18-20, NIV)

Watch enough old police shows on television, and eventually you
will encounter the cliché that "nobody is above the law." Indeed,
there is much truth to that saying. Every day, we all obey numerous
laws. Some are humanmade. Every year, I pay my taxes. I stop my
car at red lights, even when I'm the only driver on the road. Other
laws were never passed by a legislature, but most of us still obey
them. Whenever I refuse to purchase an item that I consider to be
too expensive and wait for a sale, I act in a way that confirms the law
of supply and demand. I won't be punished if I disobey, yet most of
us predictably conform to what lies in our own self-interest.

Such must surely have been the case for a young Quaker mer-
chant from Indiana named Levi Coffin (1798–1877). Coffin came
of age in a nation where the enslavement of African American men

and women was legal throughout the American South. Federal law allowed even those individuals who escaped from their bondage to be hunted down anywhere within the United States and returned to their masters. Even setting aside those Christians in America who actively supported slavery, many others made their peace with the institution and more or less ignored this great evil as they went about their everyday lives. Others spoke out, but cautiously avoided helping slaves when such assistance was deemed illegal. Few were willing to jeopardize their own self-interest in order to aid those trapped in slavery. However, Coffin sensed in his own life a calling from God to do more.

In Acts 4, the apostles Peter and John realized that even after being ordered by religious authorities not to preach in the name of Jesus, that they were bound by a higher law that required them to proclaim the gospel. In much the same way, Coffin realized that he faced a situation where human law, God's law, and his own self-interest were in conflict. And he responded in two surprising ways.

First, Coffin compromised his own business interests by joining the free produce movement. The free produce movement was an alliance of merchants and consumers who refused to deal in items produced by slave labor (such as cotton and sugar) and sought to replace them with goods manufactured by paid workers. However, merchandise produced by free labor was much more expensive than slave-made products, and Coffin's business suffered as a result.

Second, Coffin became actively involved in the Underground Railroad—so much so that he was often informally recognized as its "president." The Underground Railroad was a network of operatives and safe houses designed to help escaped slaves secretly flee the South and relocate to the relative safety of Canada. Naturally, such activities were strictly against the law. Once, while reflecting on the question of why more anti-slavery people did not directly help those slaves who were in the process of liberating themselves, Coffin observed:

> I . . . inquired of some of the Friends in our village why they did not take them in and secrete them, when they were pursued, and then aid them on their way to Canada? I found that they were afraid of the penalty of the law. I told them that I read in the Bible when I was a boy that it was right to take in the stranger and administer to those in distress, and that I thought it was always safe to do right.

More succinctly, he wrote that "the dictates of humanity came in opposition to the law of the land, and we ignored the law."

Levi Coffin stands as an example of an individual who allowed his Christian convictions to shape him both as a citizen and a consumer. The profits made in dealing in slave-made merchandise were not worth becoming economically complicit in the sin of slavery. And national laws protecting the interests of slaveholders did not excuse Coffin from his duty to sacrificially love and care for those escaping from slavery.

REFLECTION AND DISCUSSION

1. Romans 13 cautions us to "be subject to the governing authorities." How can the Bible, the church, and the larger community of believers help us discern when larger principles are at stake that might place us at odds with the government?
2. As a Quaker committed to a theology of nonviolence, Levi Coffin used acts of peace and love to confront the violence of slavery. How does Jesus' command in Matthew 5:44 ("But I tell you, love your enemies and pray for those who persecute you.") lay the foundation for Christians' struggle against evil?

FURTHER STUDY

Shortly before his death, Coffin published an autobiography entitled *Reminiscences of Levi Coffin, the Reputed President of the Underground Railroad* (available at several sites online, including https://docsouth.unc.edu/nc/coffin/coffin.html). For a very brief recent biography of Coffin, see Mary Ann Yanessa, *Levi Coffin, Quaker: Breaking the Bonds of Slavery in Ohio and Indiana.*

PRAYER

Sovereign Lord, you made the heavens and the earth and the sea, and everything in them. When nations rage, peoples plot, and rulers band against you, enable your servants to speak your word with great boldness. Amen.

(From Acts 4:24-26, 29, NIV)

All Nations

Acts 17:16-34

Sean A. Scott

> From one ancestor he made all nations to inhabit the whole earth,
> and he allotted the times of their existence and the boundaries of
> the places where they would live.
>
> (Acts 17:26)

We've all encountered someone who looked down on us based on some real or perceived superiority, maybe intellectual, athletic, or economic. Perhaps at times we've been the guilty party.

From the earliest days of Christianity, the church has struggled with this very problem. Believing Jews, heirs of the promise through Abraham, had to learn that their ethnicity did not commend them to God. To show Peter that the gospel must spread to the Gentiles, three times in a vision God commanded him to eat ceremonially unclean animals. When the Spirit led him to Cornelius the centurion, the vision's meaning became clear, and Peter professed, "I truly understand that God shows no partiality, but in every nation anyone who fears him and does what is right is acceptable to him" (Acts 10:34-35). Some Jews continued to insist that Gentiles must be circumcised to receive salvation, but at the Council of Jerusalem Peter affirmed that "in cleansing their hearts by faith [God] has made no distinction between them and us . . . On the contrary, we believe that we will be saved through the grace of the Lord Jesus, just as they will" (Acts 15:9, 11).

When Paul, the apostle to the Gentiles, traveled to Athens, the center of Greek culture and education, and preached to them that Christ was crucified and resurrected, he challenged their assumption that their intellectual and civic achievements had made them better than non-Greeks, whom they regarded as unlearned and barbaric. The sovereign Creator of the universe had made in his image all people "from one ancestor," and regardless of nationality all needed to repent in light of coming judgment (Acts 17:30-31).

The gospel's timeless message that people of all nations and language groups must come to God through repentance and faith in Christ completely levels the playing field, so that neither race, class, gender, intellect, wealth, power, nor any other factor gives one iota of advantage in gaining favor with God. This divine impartiality is a model for our human relationships as well.

African American preacher John N. Mars (1804–1884) grasped the significance of this truth better than many of his contemporaries. Born in Connecticut to parents who had escaped slavery only four years earlier, he lived among whites, enjoyed some formal education, and remembered experiencing no racial discrimination in his youth. He converted as a young adult and affiliated with the Methodists, preaching to several black congregations in New York, New England, and Canada. Yet while traveling in Maine in the early 1840s, he was denied supper aboard a steamboat despite having purchased a meal ticket. Unwilling to accept second-class status because of his skin color, he repeatedly expressed his conviction that all people are equal before God and should be treated fairly.

In fact, in 1845 he even called out President James K. Polk, who in his inaugural address had claimed a "precise equality" for all American citizens. Like a careful historian, Mars pressed the president to prove his assertion with evidence. "I hate Slavery as bad as I do the *Devil*," he wrote Polk, "and mean By the help of God to live and die a bold advocate of Equal rights to all ranks and Conditions and Colours."

Approaching his sixtieth birthday during the Civil War, Mars refused to use his advancing age as an excuse for ease. He acted out his convictions by briefly serving as a chaplain to the United States Colored Troops in North Carolina before poor health cut short his appointment. He cared so deeply for suffering freedmen and women that in 1864 he went to Portsmouth, Virginia as an agent for the American Missionary Association (AMA). He preached outdoors to sizeable crowds, started Sunday Schools, and assisted in schools for freed people. Yet some white workers apparently resisted integrated accommodations and looked down upon the blacks they taught. Seizing the opportunity for improved race relations, Mars quoted Acts 17:26 to the head of the AMA: "It is evident that God is now working out this great problem of man[']s equality and rights as given . . . by his Creator."

Mars' example of seeking racial reconciliation because of its foundation in the gospel still speaks to the church today, reminding us that God is no respecter of persons and is actively building his church from people of all tongues, tribes, and nations.

REFLECTION AND DISCUSSION

1. What specific steps can you and your local congregation take to reach out to people in your community who aren't like you?
2. Why is it important for Christians to ponder and address how past sins like racism, whether on an individual or institutional level, have hindered a faithful gospel witness and failed to portray the diversity of Christ's kingdom?

FURTHER STUDY

On African American religion and politics in the fight against slavery, try Matthew Harper's *The End of Days*. For contemporary Christian responses to racism, see Anthony B. Bradley, ed., *Aliens in the Promised Land: Why Minority Leadership Is Overlooked in White Christian Churches and Institutions*, and John Piper, *Bloodlines: Race, Cross, and the Christian*.

PRAYER

Dear Heavenly Father, you have created all people in your image, but we have marred your creation by our sin. Even as new creatures redeemed by Christ, we Christians confess that too often we show partiality. We pray that your Spirit would help us to put off our old nature with its selfish bent, and put on the new nature in Christ, which you are renewing as we grow in knowing you. For we recognize that in Christ, and in his bride the church, there are no external distinctions—neither Greek nor Jew, circumcised nor uncircumcised, barbarian, Scythian, slave, or free—but Christ is all and in all! Amen.

(Adapted from Col. 3:9-11)

"If God Is For Us"

Romans 8:26-39

Beth Allison Barr

> What then are we to say about these things? If God is for us, who
> is against us?
>
> (Rom. 8:31)

I still remember the first time I heard Chris Tomlin's song "Our
God." Our youth band was rehearsing it one night for our Wednes-
day worship service. The chorus immediately caught my attention:

> And if Our God is for us, then who could ever stop us?
> And if Our God is with us, then what can stand against?

Between 2010 and 2012, "Our God" topped Billboard's Christian
charts for 10 weeks. Chris Tomlin was named "Top Christian Artist," "Our God" won "Top Christian Song," and Chris Tomlin won
his first Grammy for the album featuring "Our God."

But these weren't the reasons the song caught my attention. It
caught my attention because of a medieval woman.

In 1433, not quite a century before the Reformation and not quite
a century after the Black Death, a woman went to hear a sermon. Her
name was Margery Kempe, and the sermon she heard changed the

course of her life. As the fifteenth-century *Book of Margery Kempe* records: "And many times [the preacher] said these words: 'If God be with us, who shall be against us?'" The medieval preacher wasn't singing like Chris Tomlin, and he certainly didn't have as large of an audience. But he was quoting the same Scripture passage that was behind Tomlin's 2010 hit: Romans 8:31.

I can almost hear the words of Chris Tomlin's twenty-first-century song echoing in the stone nave of Margery Kempe's fifteenth-century parish church.

> And if Our God is for us, then who could ever stop us?
> And if our God is with us, then what can stand against?

This Scripture passage resonated deeply with Margery Kempe, who had heard it once before. Shortly before she heard the sermon quoting Romans 8:31, Margery Kempe was sitting in church with her daughter-in-law. She felt God pressure her heart, calling her to leave England and travel to Europe. She argued with God, saying she did not have permission from her priest, that she was too old for a sea voyage, and that she didn't have the money. "She would have put it out of her mind," we read, "but ever it came again strongly so that she could have no rest or quiet in her mind, but ever was labored and commanded to go over the sea." Finally, God spoke directly to her: "If I be with thee, who shall be against thee? I shall provide for thee, and get thee friends to help thee. Do as I bid." God whispered Romans 8:31. Then God spoke those same words to her again in a sermon:

> And if Our God is for us, then who could ever stop us?
> And if our God is with us, then what can stand against?
> Then what can stand against?

Margery Kempe was advanced in age. She was mostly alone. She was defying the advice of her family. She was defying the command of her local priest. As her book records, "Some said it was a woman's whim, and a great folly . . . to put herself, a woman of great age, to the perils of the sea, and to go into a strange country where she had not been before, nor knew how she should come back."

But Margery Kempe had faith. The words of the preacher confirmed what she already believed—God wanted her "to go over the sea." So she did. Her faith took her from England to Germany; her faith carried her across the "perils of the sea" into a "strange country"; her faith carried her to pilgrim sites throughout Europe and led her to interact with people all over Europe; and then her faith brought her back home. As her book testifies, "She knew well, to God nothing was impossible."

Romans 8:31 speaks about faith. The same faith—the very same Scripture—that spoke to an American evangelical worship artist in 2010 also spoke to a medieval Catholic woman in 1433. The same faith that inspired a woman in the last part of her life to undertake an incredible journey also inspired a musician to write lyrics that would touch thousands of lives.

Sometimes the differences of our lives, the diversity of our world and our history, can seem insurmountable. I find it comforting to know that the God who never changes—the God of both Margery Kempe and Chris Tomlin—offers us the same hope today as He offered yesterday.

REFLECTION AND DISCUSSION
1. What is your legacy of faith?
2. How has God's calling changed throughout your life? Has your response to God also changed? What holds you back from answering God's call in your life?

FURTHER STUDY
You can find the video for Tomlin's song on YouTube. If you want to read *The Book of Margery Kempe*, Penguin Classics put out a paperback edition in 2000. For more on the faith of medieval women, see Ronda de Sola Chervin's *Prayers of the Women Mystics*.

PRAYER
I came to this place, Lord, for love of you. Blessed Lord, help me and have mercy on me.

(Margery Kempe)

Not Your Worry

1 Corinthians 1:18-31

Amy Collier Artman

Consider your own call, brothers and sisters: not many of you were wise by human standards, not many were powerful, not many were of noble birth. But God chose what is foolish in the world to shame the wise; God chose what is weak in the world to shame the strong; God chose what is low and despised in the world, things that are not, to reduce to nothing things that are, so that no one might boast in the presence of God.

(1 Cor. 1:26-29)

Kathryn Kuhlman was driving me crazy. I was spending hours doing research in an archive, reading about and watching video of the famous, flamboyant, and fascinating healing evangelist. Generally speaking, I enjoyed watching this female leader stride in high heels through mid-twentieth-century Christianity in America, upsetting traditional pastoral roles and social conventions while leading a thriving ministry. But then I would come across someone asking about her call from God, and she would say:

I'll tell you something very confidentially—the true conviction of my heart. I do not believe I was God's first choice in the ministry he has chosen for these last days. It's my firm conviction. You'll never argue me out of this conviction, never. I'm not quite sure whether I was God's second choice, or even His third choice . . . I was just naïve enough to say, "Take nothing, and use it." And He has been doing that ever since.

This was the answer that drove me nuts every time I read it or heard it come from Kuhlman's mouth on her television show, *I Believe in Miracles.*

On the one hand, I acknowledged the humility of her response. At its heart, the role of a disciple of Christ is one of submission to God's will. But why did she feel the need to take the further step of negating her own value and worth? Why did she have to be God's second (or third) choice?

There were many factors at play in Kuhlman's self-negation, including a savvy recognition of the contortions often necessary to be a female religious leader in the 1960s. But wasn't there a way to answer God's call on her life without degrading her own value? Does God truly require us to be *nothing* in order to use us for God's purposes?

Enter Adele Carmichael. When she joined Kuhlman on *I Believe in Miracles* in 1974, Carmichael was a respected and well-known minister in the Assemblies of God, magnificent to behold in her sparkling dress and bouffant hairdo. I remember leaning in toward the television to see what was going to happen as these two huge personalities inhabited the same sound stage. I wasn't disappointed. After general chitchat, Carmichael said to Kuhlman, "Many times I've prayed thanks that God gave you your ministry and not a man." Kuhlman responded to this surprisingly frank statement with a smile and a dismissive wave of her hand. "Really? I always thought I was second or third choice." Kuhlman surely expected this answer to be handily accepted as always. Not this time. "That's not your worry," Adele Carmichael replied crisply.

I hit pause on the ancient VCR. Here, on 1960s syndicated television, was the embodiment of two ways to respond to God's call on our lives. Kuhlman's way—to humblebrag that God was able to take our nothingness and use it—seems righteous. This way seems admirable. But is it? By refusing to believe that God could use you or me, use us fully and completely, precisely because of who we are, is a rejection of the will of God for our lives. Adele Carmichael knew this. She knew the better way: to listen for God's call on our lives and to respond with all we have and all we are, because what we have and what we are is what God wants to use.

What is God calling you to do in your life? Do you think you are able to live out that call? Do you know how much God values you as *you*? Do you realize how much you have to offer for God's use in the world?

But wait: what if you don't think you are the right one? What if you don't think you have what it takes? What if you were even God's second or third choice?

That's not your worry.

REFLECTION AND DISCUSSION

1. Do you have a story of God using you in a way you didn't expect?
2. What parts of "you" do you tend to think are not valuable to God? How could God use these "weaknesses"?
3. Do you have an Adele Carmichael in your life, a person who can remind you what is "not your worry" in your spiritual journey?

FURTHER STUDY

Want to know more about Kathryn Kuhlman? You can read my book, *The Miracle Lady*. For more about women and Pentecostal/ Charismatic Christianity, check out *Women in Pentecostal and Charismatic Ministry: Informing a Dialogue on Gender, Church, and Ministry*, coedited by Margaret English de Alminana and Lois E. Olena. And if you use Twitter, search the hashtag #womenalsoknowhistory to find more women in history or women writing history.

PRAYER

Holy One, help me to know that you can use me, all of me, for your glorious work. You can use even my weaknesses so that I can know it is truly you working in me. Thank you for being a God who validates rather than negates.

Reasonable Trust

1 Corinthians 15

Rick Kennedy

> For what I received I passed on to you as of first importance.
>
> (1 Cor. 15:3, NIV)

In his novel *Jayber Crow* (2000), Wendell Berry has Jayber, an aging village barber, reminisce:

> History grows shorter. I remember old men who remembered the Civil War. I have in my mind word-of-mouth memories more than a hundred years old. It is only twenty hundred years since the birth of Christ. Fifteen or twenty memories such as mine would reach all the way back to the halo-light in the manger at Bethlehem. So few rememberers could sit down together in a small room.

Likewise, only twenty or so people in succession separate us from the eyewitnesses to Jesus' resurrection. History is not a foreign and exotic country. The eyewitnesses to the resurrection are near. Jayber Crow is right. A small room of people is all that is needed to link us personally to the eyewitnesses.

The New Testament writers knew well that spreading the story of Jesus' resurrection throughout the world and into the future would depend on trusting eyewitness accounts and subsequent chains of hearsay rememberers. Human senses or self-evident intuition cannot communicate unique historical events. To keep alive a historical fact, Christians turned to standards established in Greek and Roman schools for the proper handling of oral and written testimony. In keeping with that classical tradition, Luke is careful at the beginning of both his Gospel and Acts to make it clear to his readers that, though he was not an eyewitness, he had interviewed eyewitnesses and investigated their stories. Paul, declaring the centrality of the historical event of the resurrection, rehearsed for his readers the critical foundation of eyewitnesses: Peter, the twelve, the "more than five hundred of the brothers and sisters at the same time, most of whom are still living," and last of all "he appeared to me also" (1 Cor. 15:5-8, NIV).

In this way Christianity is history before it is theology. It is news before it is doctrine. It is social studies before it is social science.

So too, Christianity was scribal before it was literary. Even during Jesus' life, scribes were catching his words and reporting them to employers. The gospel and letter writers of the New Testament were either eyewitnesses or early hearers of eyewitness reports who, like notaries, linked oral to written testimony. Like a deed to a property, a fact written down, attested by witnesses, holds up well through time and travels well across oceans.

One of our modern intellectual problems is that academic society has done much to downgrade the authority of eyewitnesses and responsible hearsay witnesses, both in oral and written form. Modern education enjoys teaching distrust. "Skepticism is one of the historian's finest qualities," writes Richard Marius in *A Short Guide to Writing About History*. "Historians don't trust their sources. . . . They question everything. . . . The writing of history is a brave business because good historians are willing to question all the evidence and all the assumptions." Marius recommends that the student "come to history as a doubter."

Nowhere in his book does the student get taught the reality that historians have to trust more than doubt, that history cannot be thought up like a philosophy, discovered like ancient ruins, or tested in a laboratory. History is passed among people in oral and written form. As Paul says, I pass on that which I received.

Christianity and history are both relational before they are academic. They are the stuff of people looking into each other's eyes before they are the stuff of professors, preachers, or administrators. The proper tools for history are the proper tools for a Christian. A methods course in each should begin with responsibilities and techniques of reasonable trust rather than heroic skepticism.

Three times in 1 Corinthians 15, Paul lays his cards on the table: "If Christ has not been raised then our preaching is vain, your faith also is vain" (v. 14), "if Christ has not been raised your faith is worthless; you are still in your sins" (v. 17), and by extension, "if the dead are not raised, let us eat and drink, for tomorrow we die" (v. 32, NASB). Christianity is a scribal-style history before it is theology. The resurrection, the crucial event in history, is as close as the outstretched hands of twenty or so people linked from the eyewitnesses to us.

REFLECTION AND DISCUSSION

1. As a child did you ever play a game of Telephone, in which a message is whispered from one student to another in a chain? The game is supposed to teach us how a message can be garbled as it is passed along. What would make the game more like the reality of true testimony passing through time?

2. Why is it that doubt is often thought of as heroic and safe while trust is considered naïve and risky? When is it wiser to trust than to doubt?

FURTHER STUDY

Read more about the role of eyewitness testimony in the New Testament in Richard Bauckham's *Jesus and the Eyewitnesses* and Craig Blomberg's *The Historical Reliability of the Gospels*.

PRAYER

Jesus, protect our memory of you. Encourage our trust; make our doubt wiser. Strengthen us to pass on what we have received. Amen.

The God of All Comfort

2 Corinthians 1:1-11

K. Scott Culpepper

Blessed be the God and Father of our Lord Jesus Christ, the Father of mercies and the God of all consolation, who consoles us in all our affliction, so that we may be able to console those who are in any affliction with the consolation with which we ourselves are consoled by God. For just as the sufferings of Christ are abundant for us, so also our consolation is abundant through Christ.

(2 Cor. 1:3-5)

The Apostle Paul prefaced his second epistle to the church in Corinth with a meditation on the harsh circumstances that he and his companions faced because of their desire to share the love of Christ. Paul reminded the Corinthians that it was for their sake that he suffered, but also that God's comfort was always present to strengthen him. Knowing that he was calling them to embrace a similar life of suffering for the sake of the gospel, Paul celebrated that he could rest assured that the divine comfort he experienced would be present for the Corinthians as well.

The old adage encourages us to make lemonade out of lemons. Paul urged us to make ministry out of our misery. Put with a more positive spin, we can share the comfort God gives us in times of

need with others facing similar circumstances. Just consider a story
from the early Middle Ages:

Medieval lives are veiled in mystery even under the best of circumstances. We are limited in our knowledge of even some famous
individuals by the scant sources that survive. Patrick or Patricius,
the most celebrated figure in the history of Celtic Christianity, left
few personal writings (only two ascribed to him with any certainty)
and a host of legends that make it all the more difficult to reach
the man behind them. We think that he probably lived in the late
fourth and early fifth centuries. Patrick told his personal story in the
Confessio as a defense against church officials who questioned his
testimony and ministry.

Like Paul, Patrick knew great suffering and experienced the comfort of God in his sufferings. Patrick claimed that he was kidnapped
from his home in England and taken to Ireland to be sold as a slave
when he was only sixteen. He had been ripped from a privileged
family to serve in the muck and mire of an Irish farm. The young
slave remembered the Christian teachings of his youth and began to
pray to God even though he had never been very devoted to God in
his former life. He prayed constantly and one day sensed that God
was saying he was to leave captivity. He escaped from Ireland and
returned to England after a series of adventures on the European
continent.

Patrick received a call to ministry and a visionary experience
that convinced him he must return to Ireland. Out of the crucible
of his own suffering, Patrick received comfort and strength through
his faith in Christ. His return to Ireland provided an opportunity to
share that same comfort with his former captors and fellow slaves.
Opposition was strong, but Patrick's teaching influenced a growing number of Irish converts to Christianity. As the Irish churches
grew, he established a leadership structure and encouraged a moral
renewal that included attacks on the practice of slavery among the
Irish. Not only did Patrick's influence help bring Christianity to

Ireland, but the Celtic Christian movements he inspired eventually brought the gospel back to northern Europe following the Germanic invasions of the fifth and sixth centuries.

Calling, compassion, and clarity can arise even in the midst of suffering that seems meaningless in the moment. While suffering itself is not good, Paul wrote that "all things work together for good for those who love God, who are called according to his purpose" (Rom. 8:28). The comfort we receive through Christ in the midst of our pain can open the way for us to be present for someone else in their pain. We are equipped to understand their situation in a way that others may not because of our shared experiences.

Patrick's experience as a slave deprived him of a classical Latin education, separated him from his family, imposed a life of hard labor on him, and forced him to adapt to a culture that was alien to him. Some of these things, such as his educational deficit and the Irish ways he adopted, posed barriers to his acceptance by church officials in the larger Roman Catholic Church. On the other hand, they fitted him perfectly for the role he played as "Apostle to the Irish."

REFLECTION AND DISCUSSION

1. What universal human struggles are you able to identify and confront because of your own experiences of God's grace in difficult times?
2. Who in your life today could benefit from sharing in the comfort you have received from Christ?

FURTHER STUDY

Learn more about St. Patrick and his world by reading Philip Freeman's *St. Patrick of Ireland: A Biography*. You can also read Patrick's story in his own words by reading his *Confession* in various print versions or online at https://www.confessio.ie/etexts/confessio_english#. The 2000 film *St. Patrick: The Irish Legend* offers a compelling cinematic version of Patrick's life and ministry.

PRAYER

I arise today
Through the strength of heaven;
Light of the sun,
Splendor of fire,
Speed of lightning,
Swiftness of the wind,
Depth of the sea,
Stability of the earth,
Firmness of the rock.
I arise today
Through God's strength to pilot me;
God's might to uphold me,
God's wisdom to guide me,
God's eye to look before me,
God's ear to hear me,
God's word to speak for me,
God's hand to guard me,
God's way to lie before me,
God's shield to protect me,
God's hosts to save me
Afar and anear,
Alone or in a multitude.
Christ shield me today
Against wounding
Christ with me, Christ before me, Christ behind me,
Christ in me, Christ beneath me, Christ above me,
Christ on my right, Christ on my left,
Christ when I lie down, Christ when I sit down,
Christ in the heart of everyone who thinks of me,
Christ in the mouth of everyone who speaks of me,
Christ in the eye that sees me,
Christ in the ear that hears me.
I arise today

Through the mighty strength
Of the Lord of creation.

(The anonymous "Prayer of St. Patrick" was credited to Patrick, but was probably written by an unknown Celtic Christian a century or two after his death.)

Broken Vessels

2 Corinthians 12:1-10

Dyron B. Daughrity

To keep me from being too elated, a thorn was given me in the flesh, a messenger of Satan to torment me, to keep me from being too elated. Three times I appealed to the Lord about this, that it would leave me, but he said to me, "My grace is sufficient for you, for power is made perfect in weakness." So, I will boast all the more gladly of my weaknesses, so that the power of Christ may dwell in me. Therefore I am content with weaknesses, insults, hardships, persecutions, and calamities for the sake of Christ; for whenever I am weak, then I am strong.

(2 Cor. 12:7b-10)

I love teaching church history, largely because of the fascinating personalities that pop up in each epoch. Some of these great figures are admirable because of their deep faith and their willingness to stand up for Christ. Others are beautifully in love with God, as with so many monastics and mystics. Others are important because of their lasting contributions to our collective beliefs, like the early church fathers and the trailblazing work of the early Protestant leaders. Then there are others who are famous for scandal, for brokenness, or for falling from grace.

Aimee Semple McPherson (1890–1944) is a hybrid. She was an incredible evangelist, capable of holding thousands in rapt attention by her innovative sermons. She was motivated as much for entertaining the masses as for the preaching of the gospel. It is difficult for us today to comprehend the impact this female pastor made at a time when famous women pastors were rare. In the 1920s and '30s, McPherson was among the most important Christian evangelists in the world. Virtually no one could create the media circus or attract the crowds as this homey, loveable, down-to-earth personality could. When she took the stage, the Canadian farm girl image was tossed out the window in favor of her stage persona—an electric and charismatic entertainer who could commandeer audiences, shouting Pentecostal teachings and stirring people's hearts through a combination of skilled oratory, public healings, and sheer extravagance.

McPherson accomplished more than virtually any other evangelist of her era. She founded the Foursquare Church, a Pentecostal denomination based in her beloved Los Angeles that now boasts eight million members in 144 countries. She blazed a trail for all Christian women who aspired to preach to huge crowds. She founded and built up the breathtaking Angeles Temple—America's first megachurch—in the Echo Park district of Los Angeles. Tens of millions of people came to catch a glimpse of this Holy Spirit ambassador.

Inside, however, the passionate evangelist with a heart for worldwide missions was a broken person. The woman who raised millions of dollars for the poor worked herself into a frenzy and could not find inner peace. She claimed she was kidnapped for a month in 1926. Many accused her of hiding an affair. Other allegations arose, including queries about her two very public divorces. She had a falling-out with her mother. There were whispers of various romances. Dozens of lawsuits against her. It all became too much and she succumbed to an accidental overdose of barbiturates.

Such a gifted woman. But so tempted, and so prone to give in to temptation. Yet Aimee Semple McPherson powerfully served Christ in the midst of her inner turmoil and spiritual warfare. Brilliant yet broken by Satan's penetrating thorns of the flesh, she knew the conundrum spoken of by the great apostle Paul, who considered himself the chief of sinners.

REFLECTION AND DISCUSSION
1. Why does God allow our great heroes of the faith to become so brutally tempted?
2. How is power made perfect in weakness, especially when our weaknesses include our sins?

FURTHER STUDY
There are two excellent biographies of McPherson: Matthew Avery Sutton, *Aimee Semple McPherson and the Resurrection of Christian America*, and Daniel Mark Epstein, *Sister Aimee: The Life of Aimee Semple McPherson*.

PRAYER
Father God, we are grateful for the heroes of the faith you have blessed us with. We appreciate them, listen to them, and follow them. Forgive us when we put our faith in them, however. Yet let us not condemn them. For they are often doing the best they can do, and we know that Satan is not content to let them be. Amen.

Time's Wildness

Galatians 4:1-7

Rick Kennedy

> But when the fullness of time had come, God sent his Son.
>
> (Gal. 4:4)

Historians are trained today to keep time decent and in good order. Time should line up and declare itself left to right. The Bible does not demand time to be so obedient, and Christian historians are wise to be less strict with time. The preacher warns in Ecclesiastes: "Who can make straight what [God] has made crooked?" (7:13b). The Bible pictures past, present, and future as entangled like fishing line at the bottom of the boat. John the Baptist twice says in the Gospel of John that the one coming after him existed before him. The story of salvation in the Bible is a story in which time folds back on itself like bread being kneaded. There is fullness of time in the middle. Time is like a cup overflowing. Jesus seems to say that when Moses raised a serpent on a staff, the distant future was being foretold by way of role-play.

Time is a wonder. It is not a line. It is not a circle. It cannot be described with abstract geometry. Time and distances shrink with acceleration and lengthen with deceleration. Speed, not time, is a constant in Albert Einstein's theory of relativity. The mathematician

Roger Penrose describes in his *Road to Reality* the possibility of *causality violation*, in which a signal can be sent from a future event to cause a past event.

We are all awash in the wildness of time. Yet like historians, astronomers try to domesticate time. When we look at the sky on a crisp and clear night, we experience, in one instant, millions of separate reports, delivered by millions of distinctly different light-messengers, about millions of separate moments that occurred over a range of millions of years. Time presents itself to the astronomer, as to historians, as wild. The author of my *Guide to Backyard Astronomy* notes the way most of us take such things for granted: "Nothing puzzles me more than time and space, yet nothing troubles me less."

But it should trouble us more. If reality is more complex than we normally assume, we should develop better methods of study. Richard B. Hays of Duke Divinity School titles one of his books *Reading Backwards*; on the cover he quotes John 5:46, where Jesus says that Moses wrote about him. The book is an excellent study of how improper time is in the Bible. The great struggle of Christian historians and Christian chronologists has long been the tension between keeping history tame and allowing it to express its true wildness.

One of the principal goals in the development of the modern academic discipline of history was to keep it safe. Historians should not wander in the wilderness. Carl Becker, a formative president of the American Historical Association, wrote that historians must have a past through which they can roam "with a certain sense of security." A historian, he advised, must reject some facts "not because they are contrary to every possible law of nature, to every possible experience, but simply because they are contrary to the comparative few laws of nature which his generation is willing to regard as established."

Keep history safe. That has long been a motto at the tenured center of university history departments. Focus on politics, institutions, and social issues. Avoid going too deep into biography, where a person's actual thoughts and motivations tend to be wild. "The correct answer in history courses to the question 'why,'" I recently heard an

Ivy League historian say, "is power." History should be like studying chess. Historians should not be out there roaming in the wilds of actual causes and effects.

The Bible, however, directs historians into the wild. History ceases to be only a chess game. Time becomes wholly different than any analogy we use to try to describe it. Sometimes we need to read our sources backwards. Sometimes we need to read them from the middle outward. Sometimes we need to teach our students to appreciate history the way we appreciate a multitude of stars on a crisp and clear night. Nothing is more puzzling than time and space. We need to let history be more puzzling.

REFLECTION AND DISCUSSION

1. If the Bible tells the story of salvation in such a way that "time folds back on itself like bread being kneaded," what do you think Paul means by his famous conclusion that God sent Jesus "in the fullness of time"?

2. Have you ever experienced a tension between the wildness of biblical faith and professional expectations meant to keep things "safe"?

FURTHER STUDY

Read more from Richard B. Hays in *Reading Backwards: Figural Christology and the Fourfold Gospel Witness*. You might also find interesting my own book, *Jesus, History, and Mt. Darwin: An Academic Excursion*.

PRAYER

Jesus, don't let us seek safety. Give us courage to study the wilderness of human history. Give us the wisdom to discern true causes and effects, and the humility to remember that history comes to us like the night sky. Teach us how to read backwards and discern the cup that is spilling over.

Trust in the Face of Fear

Colossians 1:15-23

Timothy L. Wood

> [The Son] is the head of the body, the church; he is the beginning
> and the firstborn from among the dead, so that in everything he
> might have the supremacy. For God was pleased to have all his
> fullness dwell in him, and through him to reconcile to himself all
> things, whether things on earth or things in heaven, by making
> peace through his blood, shed on the cross.
>
> (Col. 1:18-20, NIV)

In the 1600s, Christians often viewed the world in apocalyptic
terms. In eastern Europe, Islamic armies threatened Vienna, one
of the most important capitals in Christendom. Further west, the
Thirty Years War pitted Catholics against Protestants. In England,
conflict churned between the leaders of the established church and
Calvinistic reformers known as Puritans. Even after many of those
Puritans relocated to America, they viewed their new Native American neighbors with fear and distrust.

One way that many Christians tried to make sense of this violent
and contentious world was to assign evil motives to those outside
of their own tradition. For instance, most Protestants of the time
believed that the Roman Catholic church had fallen away from true

Christianity. Many even equated it with the Satanic forces arrayed against Christ in the Book of Revelation.

But within an atmosphere saturated with suspicion and mutual hostility, one New England minister suggested a different approach. George Philips (1593–1644) was a Puritan pastor serving a Congregationalist church in Watertown, Massachusetts. Twice (in 1631 and in a posthumous book published in 1645) Philips came forward with his opinion that the Roman Catholic church remained a true church. Certainly, real theological issues separated Catholics and Protestants in the 1600s, including the role of the papacy, faith versus works in salvation, and the role of church tradition in God's revelation to humanity. Massachusetts governor John Winthrop rebuked Philips for his unconventional opinion. However, Philips believed that it was not up to mere human beings to determine the standing of other churches before God:

> Such . . . churches, so remain true churches, so long as God continues his dispensation toward them, and no longer . . . nor is it in the power of any other church or churches, to unchurch any one such church, but Christ himself must do that.

Moreover, God's patience with these churches should inspire hope. Greater devotion often emerges when Christians come to recognize their own apathy. Repentance may follow sin. When contemplating the past, Philips remarked that it had often "pleased God more fully to cleer up the light" causing "his truth to prevail, so as many thousands were redeemed." As an example, Philips offered the Church of England, where the Puritans' own reform movement had not meant starting over, but turning to something better. The Puritan churches were not "new constituted churches" but Christian communities that were "clearing themselves from corruption, and . . . recovering themselves out of a desperate diseased condition, into a more healthful and sound estate."

George Philips lived in a frightening world where mistrust ran deep between different Christian communities and sometimes boiled over into violence. However, Philips trusted the God who transcended it all, the God whom Paul described as standing at the head of the church and reconciling all things to himself. That same God could be trusted to deal with other Christians and other churches in a way consistent with his goodness. Christ warned his disciples not to rush to judgment concerning an unknown man who was driving out demons in the name of Jesus, because God may work in ways of which we are unaware (Mark 9:38-41). Philips didn't need to understand or control that process, and understood the danger of speaking where God remained silent. The New Testament bears witness to a God who in all things providentially "works for the good of those who love him" (Rom. 8:28, NIV). For Philips, even in an era full of spiritual strife and division, that was a truth worth speaking up for.

REFLECTION AND DISCUSSION

1. Have you ever tried to deal with fear or uncertainty by "speaking for God" or judging others?
2. For you, what is the relationship between God's goodness and his trustworthiness?

FURTHER STUDY

George Philips only published one book, released a year after his death, entitled *A Reply to a Confutation of Some Grounds for Infants Baptisme: as also Concerning the Form of a Church, Put Forth Against Mee By One Thomas Lamb.* For an overview of Philips' career, see my 2011 article in *Puritan Reformed Journal*, "The Guardian of the Gathered: Covenant and Community in the Career of George Philips."

PRAYER

Father, fill us with the knowledge of your will through all the wisdom and understanding that the Spirit gives. But where we cannot understand your will, help us to trust that your Son, the head of your oft-divided church, is reconciling all things to himself. Amen.

Thanksgiving

1 Thessalonians 5:12-24

John G. Turner

Rejoice always, pray without ceasing, give thanks in all circumstances; for this is the will of God in Christ Jesus for you.

(1 Thess. 5:16-18)

Every November, just before the ill-timed break that interrupts the academic calendar, I interrupt my classes to talk about Thanksgiving. I do so in part because of my fascination with the Plymouth Colony Pilgrims, but also because the act of giving thanks is central to Christian piety and ritual.

Academic historians are good at tearing apart popular myths, and the idea of a Pilgrim's "First Thanksgiving" makes for an easy target. In a letter written for publication in England, *Mayflower* passenger Edward Winslow relates that "our harvest being gotten in, our governor sent four men on fowling, that so we might after a more special manner rejoice together, after we had gathered the fruit of our labors." The hunters had success, and the settlers feasted for a week, joined by Wampanoags who showed up after hearing their guns and then hunted deer for the occasion. The bounty was especially welcome after a winter of hunger and disease had killed half of the Pilgrims who had reached Cape Cod the previous November.

Undoubtedly, the Pilgrims were thankful, but according to the conventions of English Protestantism, the weeklong festivities were not a thanksgiving. Governments and churches proclaimed days of thanksgiving in the wake of particular blessings: a military victory, a bountiful harvest, or the resolution of a political crisis. These were rather somber affairs. Townspeople gathered in churches, sang psalms, and listened to sermons. After many hours of worship, they might then enjoy a feast and recreations. Like other Puritans, the Pilgrims rejected annual days of thanksgiving as rituals not authorized by Scripture. They would find the late-November Thanksgiving of the early twenty-first-century United States utterly abhorrent.

It is easy to poke holes in popular ideas about the past, but it is more instructive to move beyond deconstruction. There were many days of thanksgiving during the seventy-year history of Plymouth Colony. In 1623, Governor William Bradford appointed a day of fasting and prayer during a drought, then a day of thanksgiving after heavy rains. In December 1636, the town of Scituate observed a day of thanksgiving. Townspeople gathered at half past eight on a frigid day and worshiped for four hours, "then making merry to the creatures, the poorer sort invited of the richer." While few Americans would feel thankful to sit in a cold church for hours, we could do worse than to imitate the way that Scituate's more prosperous citizens practiced hospitality. There are also some less savory Plymouth Colony thanksgivings, namely those times when settlers thanked God for victories over Native peoples, victories that contributed to the dispossession and subjugation of New England's Indian communities.

God commands Christians to give thanks, not on the fourth Thursday in November, nor on particular days after unusual blessings. "Rejoice always," Paul instructs the church in Thessalonica, "pray without ceasing, give thanks in all circumstances." I tell my students that this is a hard commandment. Human circumstances, for Christians and for others, are so disparate. There are times to mourn and times to dance, teaches the Book of Ecclesiastes. Yet Paul insists that it is God's will that Christians give thanks regardless of those circumstances.

I then point my students—and myself—to a passage in Augustine's *Confessions*. The Bishop of Hippo thanks God for all of the gifts received in his childhood, including the growing recognition of his own sinfulness. "I would still thank you even if you had not willed me to live beyond boyhood," Augustine reflects. He prays that God will perfect those gifts, and he writes with a faith that whenever he dies, he will be with God. "This too is your gift to me," Augustine finishes his prayer, "that I exist."

For Christians, being thankful is not the same thing as being happy, which is sometimes impossible. Rather, through Jesus Christ we belong to God in all of the circumstances of life, and even in death. That is a firm foundation for Christian thanksgiving.

REFLECTION AND DISCUSSION

1. Paul instructs Christians to rejoice, pray, and give thanks constantly. Is this hyperbole, or a reasonable teaching?
2. When things go well in our lives, do we attribute it to fortune, our own efforts, or to God?

FURTHER STUDY

The richest portrait of the Plymouth Pilgrims is Jeremy Dupertuis Bangs, *Strangers and Pilgrims, Travellers and Sojourners: Leiden and the Foundations of Plymouth Plantation*. For a reflection on the Pilgrims and thanksgiving, see Robert Tracy McKenzie's *The First Thanksgiving: What the Real Story Tells Us About Loving God and Learning from History*.

PRAYER

I give thanks to you, my sweetness, my honor, my confidence; to you, my God, I give thanks for your gifts. Do you preserve them for me. So will you preserve me too, and what you have given me will grow and reach perfection, and I will be with you; because this too is your gift to me—that I exist.

(Augustine of Hippo)

"A Great Cloud of Witnesses" and the "Modesto Manifesto"

Hebrews 12:1-3

Grant Wacker

> Therefore, since we are surrounded by such a great cloud of witnesses, let us throw off everything that hinders and the sin that so easily entangles. And let us run with perseverance the race marked out for us.
>
> (Heb. 12:1, NIV)

Christian historians love the opening of this passage—"we are surrounded by such a great cloud of witnesses"—for it gives the validation of Scripture to our line of work. More precisely, it seems to turn our jobs into real vocations. To adapt the final haunting lines of Willa Cather's great novel, *My Antonia*, the great cloud of witnesses helps us to possess together "the precious, the incommunicable past"—which is to say, it helps us come home to ourselves as Christians.

And so it is that we are called to summon our readers to pay attention to the wisdom of the ages. We did not create ourselves. Theology—in the broadest sense of the word, as the authoritative rationale for all that we say and do as Christians—comes to us, not as a sacred meteor, dropping from the sky, unbidden and unannounced, but rather as the time-tested sagacity of the church. That wisdom helps us differentiate our own ideas, if not whims, from the settled interpretations of the church's past, interpretations that have been refined in the fire of experience.

The next clause receives less attention: "let us throw off the sin that hinders and the sin that so easily entangles." This is hard medicine. The injunction is not just to subordinate, not even to discipline, but to throw off. Historically, evangelicals have given themselves a pass on this short but weighty passage by targeting the sins that few were committing anyway—smoking, drinking, dancing, cussing, fornication. But believers found that the broader and deeper behavior patterns that demanded attention were excised with more difficulty.

For evangelicals, especially, one of the chief blueprints for throwing off the sin that entangles was articulated in 1949 by Billy Graham and three of his associates. It came to be known as the "Modesto Manifesto" because it was created in a motel room in that California city after the four men had prayed and talked about the pitfalls that had destroyed other evangelists' ministries. They boiled the pitfalls down to four: financial deceit, sexual immorality, misleading reports, and incivility toward others (especially critics). Graham never called it the "Modesto Manifesto," and it was never written up in the form of an official document. But it took on a life of its own.

As it happened, the second prescription, sexual morality, took on a life of *its* own. It came to be known simply as the Billy Graham Rule: never travel or dine alone with a woman who was not a family member. For Graham, that was just a matter of common sense. The prescription was designed to serve as a fence around himself, not others. A young man in the prime of life, he knew his own vulnerabilities. The goal was to avoid tempting situations in the first place.

To be sure, moral and ethical guidelines for daily life, however high-minded in intent, often run into complications in practice. Over time "The Rule" has undoubtedly borne unforeseen results, sometimes excluding women from leadership venues and sometimes casting a shadow over their personal integrity. But that is another story. The relevant point just now is Graham's recognition that Christians should seek a life freed from "the sin that hinders" in every way possible. For him integrity, chastity, truthfulness, and civility ranked as markers of a journey committed to Christ, in accord with the testimony of the church.

But what about the conclusion of that first verse in Hebrews 12: "let us run with perseverance the race marked out for us"? Scripture leaves no doubt that moral misdemeanors—fudging on accounting, borderline flirtations, exaggerations about accomplishments, sharp words in defense of Truth—readily lead to moral felonies such as cheating, adultery, lies, and violence. Moreover, appearances count. Avoiding sin also means avoiding the behavior that gives rise to perceptions of sin. Translated into today's scene, this means that "what happens in Las Vegas"—as the television commercial goes—does *not* stay in Las Vegas. Rather it bears ramifications for how the Body of Christ is perceived everywhere.

Where does this well-trodden passage from Hebrews leave us? Do moral misdemeanors—whether occasional or habitual—tarnish the Christian life? Yes, of course. Do they always lead to moral felonies? No, of course not. But common experience tells us that they often do. Does grace protect us from temptations? No. Is vigilance required? Yes.

Does God's grace redeem the record of our lives, and invigorate us with strength for the journey, just as it has invigorated the great cloud of witnesses since time immemorial? Yes, again. And for that, we offer thanks.

REFLECTION AND DISCUSSION

1. How does the study of the Christian past—the cloud of witnesses—offer moral examples of lives well-lived, not perfectly, but consistently aboveboard and beyond reproach?

2. What sorts of situations call for common sense judgments not only about absolute standards of right and wrong but also about how the church is best served?

FURTHER STUDY

For more on Billy Graham, try William Martin's *A Prophet with Honor* or my own book, *One Soul at a Time*. For further reflection on moral living, see Lewis Smedes, *What God Expects from Ordinary People*.

PRAYER

Lord, we seek guidance. In your bounty you have given us a cloud of witnesses, faithful men and women who in times past have navigated the complications of daily life, just as we do today. Their example offers wisdom and strength. We also seek understanding for knowing the importance of boundaries: knowing when, where, and how to draw them. Toward these ends enlighten our minds, strengthen our hands, and open our hearts.

"Living Hope"

1 Peter 1:3-9

John Fea

> Blessed be the God and Father of our Lord Jesus Christ! By
> his great mercy he has given us a new birth into a living hope
> through the resurrection of Jesus Christ from the dead, and into
> an inheritance that is imperishable, undefiled, and unfading, kept
> in heaven for you, who are being protected by the power of God
> through faith for a salvation ready to be revealed in the last time.
>
> (1 Pet. 1:3-5)

I recently visited the old Ebenezer Baptist Church in Atlanta, the
church where Martin Luther King Jr. was baptized and where
he served as pastor. King's final sermon, the one he delivered on
April 3, 1968, was playing over the speakers. The civil rights activist
was in Memphis to encourage sanitation workers fighting for better
pay and improved working conditions. I sat in the back pew and
listened to the recording:

> Well, I don't know what will happen now. We've got some difficult
> days ahead. But it really doesn't matter with me now. Because I've
> been to the mountaintop. And I don't mind. Like anybody, I would
> like to live a long life. Longevity has its place. But I'm not concerned
> about that now. I just want to do God's will. And He has allowed
> me to go up the mountain. And I've looked over, and I've seen the

Promised Land. I may not get there with you, but I want you to know
tonight, that we as a people will get to the Promised Land. So I'm
happy tonight. I'm not worried about anything. I'm not fearing any
man. Mine eyes have seen the glory of the coming of the Lord.

It was a message of hope. Because King had been born anew to
a "living hope through the resurrection of Jesus Christ from the
dead," he awaited a glorious inheritance. Because of his faith, God
had given him all the strength he needed to continue to endure the
suffering that came with his trial. King had made himself available
to do the Lord's will. Now he was looking forward. An assassin's bul-
let took his life the next day, but the movement went on.

In an age in which politicians, pundits, and even some Christian
leaders appeal to our fears, Peter exhorts us in this epistle to have
hope. The historian Christopher Lasch once wrote, "Hope does not
demand a belief in progress. It demands a belief in justice: a conviction that the wicked will suffer, that wrongs will be made right, that
the underlying order of things is not flouted with impunity. Hope
implies a deep-seated trust in life that appears absurd to most who
lack it."

This kind of hope will always appear foolish to an onlooking
world. But Peter reminds us that such hope brings life—the promise
of a new heaven and a new earth (2 Pet. 3:13). It brings expectation,
longing, and joy amid a broken world. Even when the times seem
to suggest that there is little to be optimistic about, we can still have
hope. We know by faith that history is on our side.

The stains of sin are everywhere. We lament over the world's long
history of racism, inequality, nativism, violence, and tyranny. We tell
stories about the past to illuminate these injustices so that we don't
repeat our mistakes. But every now and then, God's kingdom—a
kingdom defined by love, mercy, compassion, and justice—breaks
through and we get a glimpse of the imperishable, undefiled, and
unfading inheritance that awaits us. These stories, which historians
also need to tell, remind us that time will one day consummate in
the Kingdom of God.

REFLECTION AND DISCUSSION

1. What stories—past or present—give you a glimpse into the coming inheritance promised to those who have been "born anew to a living hope"?
2. How does the hope Peter talks about in this passage offer a rebuke to a life defined by fear?

FURTHER STUDY

On the civil rights movement as a religious movement, see David Chappell, *A Stone of Hope: Prophetic Religion and the Death of Jim Crow*. On hope, see N. T. Wright, *Surprised by Hope: Rethinking Heaven, the Resurrection, and the Mission of the Church*.

PRAYER

Pardon for sin and a peace that endureth,
Thine own dear presence to cheer and to guide,
Strength for today and bright hope for tomorrow,
Blessings all mine, with ten thousand beside!
Great is Thy faithfulness!
Great is Thy faithfulness!
Morning by morning new mercies I see:
All I have needed Thy hand hath provided—
Great is Thy Faithfulness, Lord, unto me!

(Thomas O. Chisholm, "Great Is Thy Faithfulness")

Christian Historians Are Priests Called to Spend Their Lives on Others

1 Peter 2:1-10

Douglas A. Sweeney

> Come to him, a living stone, though rejected by mortals yet chosen and precious in God's sight, and like living stones, let yourselves be built into a spiritual house, to be a holy priesthood, to offer spiritual sacrifices acceptable to God through Jesus Christ.
>
> (1 Pet. 2:4-5)

Today more than ever, Christians all across the globe—Catholic, Protestant, and Orthodox—are united in support of the priestly work of the laity. Most Protestants associate this emphasis with Martin Luther, who developed it in opposition to Roman Catholic teaching on the higher Christian life lived by priests, monks, and nuns. On the basis of Scripture texts like the one quoted above, he taught that "every baptized Christian is a priest already, not by appointment or ordination . . . but because Christ himself has begotten him as a priest and has given birth to him in Baptism." But nearly all Christians now agree that those who follow Jesus share in the Lord's priestly ministry and play an important role in spreading his love and grace in the world. This was codified, in fact, at the Second Vatican Council.

Nowhere is this priesthood more necessary today than in the realm of education, which is full of fragile egos, insecurities, uncertainties, and fears—to say nothing of most of the ordinary forms of human suffering. Our schools, colleges, universities, and seminaries are full of sinners standing in need of grace and mercy, people plagued by doubts and debts but still expected to perform as confident masters of their subjects and magnanimous public figures. These pressures breed anxiety and toxic self-absorption, yielding a morally repugnant blend of obsequiousness toward those whom we assume can ease our burden and obliviousness, or even disrespect, to those who cannot.

In the midst of this situation, Christian historians share a special calling to worldly ministry, to live as priests among our neighbors in the guild. We share a mandate from the Bible to serve in the manner of Jesus Christ, whose life was spent for people like us in humble, self-defeating love. As depicted by St. Paul in his epistle to the Philippians, this mandate reads as follows:

> Do nothing from selfish ambition or conceit, but in humility regard others as better than yourselves. Let each of you look not to your own interests, but to the interests of others. Let the same mind be in you that was in Christ Jesus, who, though he was in the form of God, did not regard equality with God as something to be exploited, but emptied himself, taking the form of a slave, being born in human likeness. And being found in human form, he humbled himself and became obedient to the point of death—even death on a cross. (2:3-8)

Without confusing our secular roles with those of officially ordained priests, or assuming the weighty mantle of ecclesial authority, we are nonetheless to engage in acts of sacrificial service to our colleagues in the field. We are to make time for others, put their needs before our own, support their academic labors, and rejoice in their success.

We are to help them interpersonally, demonstrating compassion for their welfare in the world.

In an era characterized by academic acquisitiveness, we are called to model a countercultural *modus operandi*. Rather than spending so much time attracting attention to ourselves, trying desperately to impress, and practicing scholarly one-upmanship, we are called to build up others, valorizing their achievements. Rather than trying quite so hard to be players in the academy, win respect from those in power, and demonstrate to others that Christians are not as dumb as they seem, we are called to be "poor in spirit," to "hunger and thirst for righteousness," to be "pure in heart," and "salt" and "light" in the world (Matt. 5:1-16). We are also called to witness to the "foolishness" of history (1 Cor. 1–2), calling things as we see them through the spectacles of faith. Rather than holding back for fear that other scholars will reject us, it is time to reach out and face the consequences of faith, hope, and love within the academy.

It is time to shower attention on those who have no power over us, meeting the needs of junior colleagues and students before we tend to our C.V.'s, and looking for ways to treat others—especially "the least" of those among us—as though they were better, more important, than ourselves. It is time to tell the truth—the whole truth—about our work, "outing" ourselves as Christians when the occasion calls for it. We need not drive away our colleagues with annoying, artificial attempts to make a Christian difference, substituting spiritual chatter or religious moralism for painstaking scholarship. But we *do* need to resist the many professional enticements, institutional incentives, and pecuniary tugs to live as scholarly Nicodemites, practicing Christian faith by night but failing to show ourselves, or be ourselves, by day.

As historian Kenneth E. Hagin wrote of Luther's view of calling, "The vocation of love, serving the neighbor, is not optional. The whole structure of God's world is ordered so that the neighbor is served in and by vocation." May God help us as we seek to spend our lives on those around us with faithful, hopeful, and loving priestly ministry.

REFLECTION AND DISCUSSION

1. Do you think of yourself as a priest? Why, or why not?
2. What difference might this notion make in your everyday life as a student, a disciple, a budding scholar, or a practicing historian?

FURTHER STUDY

The classic source on Luther's doctrine of the vocation of believers is Gustaf Wingren, *Luther on Vocation*, trans. Carl C. Rasmussen. For a shorter and more lucid introduction to "Luther on Vocation," see Karlfried Froehlich's 1999 essay by that title in *Lutheran Quarterly*.

PRAYER

Dear Father in Heaven, for the sake of your dear Son Jesus Christ grant us your Holy Spirit, that we may be true learners of Christ, and therefore acquire a heart with a never-ceasing fountain of love. Amen.

(Martin Luther)

"From All Tribes and Peoples"

Revelation 7

Jay R. Case

> After this I looked, and there was a great multitude that no one
> could count, from every nation, from all tribes and peoples and
> languages, standing before the throne and before the Lamb,
> robed in white, with palm branches in their hands.

(Rev. 7:9)

At three critical historical moments in the biblical narrative, we find
the term "nation." First, God establishes his covenant with Abraham
by promising him that "you shall be the ancestor of a multitude of
nations" (Gen. 17:4). The second key moment occurs right after the
resurrection, when Christ appears to the disciples and tells them to
"go therefore and make disciples of all nations" (Matt. 28:19). We
find the third instance in the book of Revelation, when John sees
the countless multitude before the Lamb on the throne, a multitude
"from every nation." In its barest form—from Abraham to Christ to
that future point around the throne—this is the historical structure
of God's redemptive purposes for humanity.

What, then, is meant by "nation"? We know, at first glance,
that the use of "nation" in these passages indicates that the gospel
is for everyone. We know that all humans are addressable by God,

accountable to God, and have dignity because they are made in the image of God.

But there is more. "Nation" is used in a way that indicates God does not intend to transform humanity into one uniform, homogeneous culture. After all, God said he would make Abraham an ancestor of many nations, not that he would bring all people into one nation under Abraham.

Solid scholarship on the history of Christianity deepens this point. This devotional, for instance, gives us a tiny glimpse of the Kingdom of God at work in a range of different settings. From St. Patrick's sufferings, to Huguenot refugees arriving in strange places, to the gifts of women in patriarchal settings, to the tragedy of the Holocaust, to justice-seeking civil rights workers, we see Christ meeting people in their specific cultural situation, working out his redemptive purposes amidst a sinful humanity, and bringing blessings to the world.

Furthermore, Christian scholars in the last few decades have started to come to terms with something we now call "world Christianity." The center of gravity of Christianity in the past century has shifted from Europe and North America to Africa, Asia, and Latin America. Not only do Christians in each of these major global areas now outnumber all Americans, we find hundreds and thousands of different cultural variations in each region. In fact, this shift has refocused historians' attention on the distant past, to help us see that even from its inception, Christianity was never solely a Western religion.

The late Lamin Sanneh, a Christian theologian born and raised a Muslim in West Africa, has unpacked an important dynamic of world Christianity: translation. He points out that Muslims believe the Qur'an must be read or spoken in classical Arabic in order for its full sacred character to be understood. As a result, Islam tends to pull Muslims to the center of Arabic culture. The Bible, however, can be translated into any language and still retain its sacred character. Something deeply incarnational takes place: Christ speaks the language of anybody who hears the Word. Their language and their culture prove to be worthy vessels of Christ's glory.

When we consider the role of "nations" in Scripture and history, then, we discover a certain kind of diversity inherently built into God's plan for redemption. This is not a shallow diversity in which we simply hold polite conversations with others before retreating back to our safe and familiar spaces, like we were sampling foods at an ethnic festival before returning to our homes. Nor is it a soft and complacent diversity in which we do nothing more than celebrate differences that we find acceptable in each other, hiding our faces from the unjust, sinful, and broken components in our own culture and in others. It is not the diversity of full-blown moral relativism, where everyone decides for themselves what is good and true—a diversity that is actually built upon Western individualism.

Instead, this diversity is built upon Christ's delight in his human creation and his loving desire to redeem that humanity. It is a diversity built into the promise given to Abraham, a promise that will reach fulfillment on that day when we will find ourselves gathered around the throne of the Lamb, rejoicing with multitudes of people from every nation.

REFLECTION AND DISCUSSION

1. In what ways does God call us, like Christ, to meet others on their own cultural terms?
2. What practices and habits do we have, individually or collectively, that tempt us to engage only those who are similar to ourselves?

FURTHER STUDY

To think afresh about the Christian mission and world Christianity in the early twenty-first century, I'd recommend starting with Lamin Sanneh, *Translating the Message: The Missionary Impact on Culture*; Andrew F. Walls, *The Missionary Movement in Christian History: Studies in the Transmission of Faith*; and Christopher J. H. Wright, *The Mission of God: Unlocking the Bible's Grand Narrative*.

PRAYER

O Lord, may we see everyone, regardless of who they are, as people made in your image. Give us a deeper, greater, and fuller picture of your purposes for humanity, in all its diversity.

Further Resources

You can follow the Conference on Faith and History on Twitter and Facebook, and many of its members are active on social media and the blogosphere. Several contributors to this devotional write about "the relevance of religious history for today" at *The Anxious Bench* (www.patheos.com/blogs/anxiousbench). John Fea and Chris Gehrz blog regularly at *The Way of Improvement Leads Home* (thewayofimprovement.com) and *The Pietist Schoolman* (pietistschoolman.com), respectively.

Fea, Gehrz, and Jemar Tisby also host podcasts, further examples of how historians are exploring the possibilities of that digital medium. *BackStory, Ben Franklin's World, Hardcore History, The Memory Palace, More Perfect, Past Present, Presidential, Throughline,* and *Uncivil* are among the many other fine options available for download or streaming.

Several CFH members have authored helpful reflections on how Christians study the past: e.g., Margaret Bendroth, *The Spiritual Practice of Remembering*; John Fea, *Why Study History? Reflecting on the Importance of the Past*; Jay Green, *Christian Historiography: Five Rival Versions*; and Robert Tracy McKenzie, *A Little Book for New Historians: Why and How to Study History*. Mark Noll considers the relationship between Christology and history in chapter five of *Jesus Christ and the Life of the Mind*.

Online you can find more coverage of the history of Christianity at *Christian History Magazine* (christianhistoryinstitute.org) and *Christianity Today* (christianitytoday.com/history). For popular history writing online that goes beyond the church, see *Smithsonian Magazine* (smithsonianmag.com/history) and *History Today* (historytoday.com).

Contributors

Amy Collier Artman is on the Religious Studies faculty at Missouri State University in Springfield, Missouri. She is the author of *The Miracle Lady: Kathryn Kuhlman and the Transformation of Charismatic Christianity.* *(1 Corinthians)*

Beth Allison Barr is associate dean in the graduate school and associate professor of history at Baylor University. An expert on medieval women's history, her most recent book is *The Making of Biblical Womanhood.* *(Matthew, Romans)*

Margaret Bendroth, who served as executive director of the Congregational Library and Archives in Boston, Massachusetts from 2004 to 2020, is a historian of religion specializing in twentieth-century American Protestantism. *(Matthew)*

Mary R. S. Bracy is an independent scholar and consultant based in Tampa, Florida. *(Isaiah)*

Jared S. Burkholder is professor of history at Grace College in Winona Lake, Indiana. He serves on the editorial board of the *Journal of Moravian History* and is the editor of *Brethren Intersections: History, Identity, Crosscurrents.* *(Matthew)*

Joel Carpenter is a senior research fellow with the Nagel Institute for the Study of World Christianity, at Calvin University. His most recent book, coedited with Rebecca Shah, is *Christianity in India: Conversion, Community Development, and Religious Freedom. (1 Kings)*

Heath W. Carter is associate professor of American Christianity at Princeton Theological Seminary. He is the author of *Union Made: Working People and the Rise of Social Christianity in Chicago* and the coeditor of three other books. *(Matthew)*

Jay R. Case is professor of history at Malone University in Canton, Ohio. He is finishing a book, tentatively entitled *The Shift*, that takes a historical and theological look at the way world Christianity has affected Christianity in the United States. *(Matthew, Revelation)*

Elesha Coffman is associate professor of history at Baylor University and editor of *Fides et Historia*, the journal of the Conference on Faith and History. *(Exodus)*

K. Scott Culpepper is professor of history at Dordt University in Sioux Center, Iowa. He is currently writing on the influence of "spiritual warfare" beliefs on American political and popular cultures. *(2 Corinthians)*

Dyron B. Daughrity is professor of religion at Pepperdine University in Malibu, California. He also serves as pastor of the Pasadena Church of Christ. *(2 Corinthians)*

Jonathan Den Hartog is professor of history and department chair at Samford University in Birmingham, Alabama. He is the author of *Patriotism and Piety: Federalist Politics and Religious Struggle in the New American Nation. (Ecclesiastes)*

Lisa Clark Diller is professor of early modern history at Southern Adventist University in Chattanooga, Tennessee. She writes and speaks on the contribution of religious minorities to ideas of citizenship, justice, and toleration. *(Leviticus)*

Janine Giordano Drake is clinical assistant professor of history at Indiana University (Bloomington). She is currently completing a manuscript on the American rivalry for moral and spiritual authority between the churches and the labor movement. *(Leviticus)*

Kristin Kobes Du Mez is professor of history at Calvin University in Grand Rapids, Michigan. Her most recent book is *Jesus and John Wayne: How White Evangelicals Corrupted a Faith and Fractured a Nation. (Luke)*

John Fea is professor of history at Messiah College in Mechanicsburg, Pennsylvania. He is the author of several books, including *Why Study History? Reflecting on the Importance of the Past.* *(1 Peter)*

Christopher Gehrz is professor of history at Bethel University in St. Paul, Minnesota. The author or editor of three books on Pietism, he is currently writing a spiritual biography of aviator Charles A. Lindbergh. *(Genesis, Luke)*

Verónica A. Gutiérrez is associate professor of Latin American history at Azusa Pacific University in Azusa, California, where she also serves as Director of Undergraduate Research. She is currently writing the first history of early colonial Cholula, Mexico. *(Jeremiah)*

Karen J. Johnson is associate professor of history at Wheaton College in Wheaton, Illinois. She works on the intersection of religion and race in U.S. history. *(Amos)*

Rick Kennedy is professor of history at Point Loma Nazarene University in San Diego, California and secretary to the Conference on Faith and History. He is the author of *The First American Evangelical: A Short Life of Cotton Mather.* *(1 Corinthians, Galatians)*

Darin D. Lenz is associate professor of history at Fresno Pacific University in California. He earned his Ph.D. under the supervision of Robert D. Linder, founding editor of the Conference on Faith and History journal, *Fides et Historia.* *(Joshua)*

Shivraj K. Mahendra is a Ph.D. candidate at Asbury Theological Seminary in Wilmore, Kentucky. He is the history editor at the Asian American Theological Forum and graduate student representative at the Conference on Faith and History. *(Psalms)*

David McFarland is a high school history teacher at Pacific Academy in Surrey, British Columbia. In addition to cohosting a podcast on K–12 Christian teaching and learning, he is currently studying at Fuller Theological Seminary. *(Amos)*

Shirley A. Mullen is president of Houghton College. She is working on a book of essays on the centrality of historical thinking to a liberal arts philosophy of education. *(Psalms)*

Mark A. Noll is Francis A. McAnaney Professor of History Emeritus at the University of Notre Dame. He has recently published a second edition of *A History of Christianity in the United States and Canada*. *(Psalms)*

Rick Ostrander is a higher education consultant who helps private colleges and universities become more innovative and collaborative. *(Matthew)*

Amy L. Poppinga is associate professor of history at Bethel University (MN). She is involved in research, teaching, and community service related to interfaith engagement. *(Genesis)*

Trisha Posey is professor of history and director of the Honors Scholars Program at John Brown University in Siloam Springs, Arkansas. Her areas of research include religion, slavery, and race in the nineteenth-century United States. *(Psalms)*

Wendy Wong Schirmer received her Ph.D. in Early American history. She currently teaches Intellectual Heritage at Temple University. *(Luke)*

Brenda Thompson Schoolfield is professor of history at Bob Jones University in Greenville, South Carolina. She serves as chair of the Division of History, Government, and Social Science. *(Ruth, Joel)*

Sean A. Scott is assistant professor of history at the Indiana Academy for Science, Mathematics, and Humanities. *(Acts)*

David R. Swartz is associate professor of history at Asbury University in Wilmore, Kentucky. He is the author of *Facing West: American Evangelicals in an Age of World Christianity* and *Moral Minority: The Evangelical Left in an Age of Conservatism*. *(John)*

Lisa Weaver-Swartz is an independent scholar and a lecturer in sociology at Asbury University. Her forthcoming book, *Gendered Gospels: Male Power, Women's Voice, and Evangelical Authority*, explores the gendered dynamics of evangelical seminaries. *(Exodus)*

Douglas A. Sweeney is dean and professor of divinity at Beeson Divinity School, Samford University. He has written widely on early modern Protestant history and global evangelicalism. *(1 Peter)*

Jemar Tisby is a Ph.D. candidate at the University of Mississippi, the president of The Witness, a Black Christian Collective, and author of *The Color of Compromise: The Truth about the American Church's Complicity in Racism*. *(Mark)*

John G. Turner is professor of religious studies at George Mason University. His latest book is *They Knew They Were Pilgrims: Plymouth Colony and the Contest for American Liberty*. *(1 Thessalonians)*

Andrea L. Turpin is associate professor of history at Baylor University. She is the author of *A New Moral Vision: Gender, Religion, and the Changing Purposes of American Higher Education, 1837–1917*. *(Nehemiah)*

Grant Wacker is Gilbert T. Rowe Professor Emeritus of Christian History at Duke Divinity School. He recently authored *One Soul at a Time: The Story of Billy Graham*. *(Hebrews)*

Daniel K. Williams is professor of history at the University of West Georgia. He is the author of *God's Own Party: The Making of the Christian Right* and *Defenders of the Unborn: The Pro-Life Movement before Roe v. Wade*. *(Luke)*

Nadya Williams is associate professor of history at the University of West Georgia. She is the coeditor of *Civilians and Warfare in World History*, and is currently writing a book on St. Augustine's philosophy of history. *(Proverbs)*

Timothy L. Wood is the Roy Blunt Professor of History at Southwest Baptist University in Bolivar, Missouri, where he serves as chair of the Department of History and Political Science. He is the author of *Agents of Wrath, Sowers of Discord: Authority and Dissent in Puritan Massachusetts, 1630–55*. *(Acts, Colossians)*

CPSIA information can be obtained
at www.ICGtesting.com
Printed in the USA
LVHW021646300121
677906LV00002B/118